Travel the Lewis and Clark Trail from South Dakota to Oregon

Mary Vasudeva

ACKNOWLEDGMENTS

A special thanks to Vive and to Roads Scholar

Contents

(all map credits are indicated at the end of the book)

Introduction

Lewis and Clark have intrigued travelers for over two centuries. And whether you are a Lewis and Clark "groupie", someone who might enjoy stopping at a site or two on an upcoming trip, or an armchair traveler interested in a "rediscovery" of the corps' exploration, this book provides visitor information and historical and cultural touchstones for Lewis and Clark's travels from South Dakota to the Pacific and back. Obviously, in the 200+ years that have passed since their 1804-1806 expedition much of the land has changed, and, in many cases, the site the corps visited itself is literally gone, often under water. But the route itself remains, and this guide provides an opportunity to "rediscover" the corps' footsteps.

But before we hit the SE tip of South Dakota for our journey, we have to quickly return to Washington D.C., to Thomas Jefferson who initiated and supported the expedition.

Jefferson's Corp of Discovery

Thomas Jefferson, our nation's third president, was fascinated with exploration and the vast unknown West, especially after the Louisiana Purchase in 1803. To add to his already ardent desire to know more about this territory, Jefferson had recently read Scottish explorer Alexander MacKenzie's book, Voyages from Montreal, on exploring the area from the continental divide in what is now Canada through British Columbia. Jefferson feared that if America did not commandeer the territory from the American frontier to the Pacific some other country would. In addition, the idea of a mythical Northwest passage that would take Easterners to the pacific was constantly in mind. For decades, the belief that travelers could go easily by water from east to west had been perpetuated but never substantiated. An expedition was surely necessary to confirm and map the route.

Jefferson believed strongly in the power of knowledge, particularly scientific knowledge. Such knowledge, he argued, was not for his own or even government's edification but to share with everyone. This knowledge would be America's knowledge. It was quite a vision for our future. And, his forward-thinking benefits all of us today. That we can follow Lewis and Clark across America over 200 years after their journey, continuing to learn from their experiences, is not just a pleasure for the curious traveler but an education in history, culture, astronomy, geology, weather, geography, nature and people. It is not an exaggeration to say that the corps of discovery was the most significant exploration on the American continent.

> Lewis' Library
>
> Lewis received significant tutoring before he departed on his journey from everyone from his mother who taught him herbal medicine to Andrew Ellicott, Secretary of the Land Office, who taught him map making. From Robert Patterson, a Mathematics and Natural Philosophy professor at University of Pennsylvania, who worked with Lewis on math, to Casper Wistar, Professor of Anatomy at University of Pennsylvania, who helped him to identify fossils. Apparently, Lewis was a quick study, and he was able to apply his skills in the field. He also brought a small library with him to facilitate and aid his own knowledge. It is believed that he brought Patrick Kelly's A Practical Introduction of Spherics and Nautical Astronomy (1796), The Nautical Almanac and Astronomical Ephemeris (1767), a book used to calculate latitude and longitude, Benjamin Barton's Elements of Botany (1803), John Miller's two-volume set, An Illustration of the Sexual System of Linnaeus (1779) which highlighted Linnean classification, and Elements of Mineralogy (1784) by Richard Kirwan. It is believed that Lewis and Clark might have brought along a couple of additional books including Voyages from Montreal, the book that greatly influenced Jefferson's desire to explore the route west.

Why This Guide?

This trail guide provides essential information about places to visit that interpret the Lewis and Clark trail and The Corps of Discovery spanning from South Dakota to the Pacific Ocean. Generally, the places are listed in their geographical order on the trail as Lewis and Clark followed it. While this is not in chronological order, it is more logical to follow geographical order because they traversed the same or similar spots going out and coming back, and, thus, it would be repetitive to include them chronologically.

Most of us heard about Lewis and Clark in American history lessons throughout our schooling, but getting an up-close look at their travels provides a much more memorable and engaging opportunity to learn about one of the foremost explorations in history. What makes this journey even more memorable is just how off the beaten path many of these destinations are. As you trek to some of the furthest of the Lewis and Clark sites, you can't help but marvel at their tenacity and grit. It's hard to imagine the trip with no transportation but feet and boats (and imagine carrying the boats whenever they had to portage), no coolers, no guides, no GPS, no maps, just ambition, courage and a belief that what they were doing would benefit the entire country. The success of the journey given the obstacles and struggles continues to amaze.

Gates of the Mountains

Further Exploration

If you have the time, it's worthwhile to watch the PBS Ken Burns production of the expedition: *Lewis and Clark: The Journey of the Corps of Discovery.* It's available at Amazon or on PBS' website. The 240 minute film provides a thorough introduction to the trip, and is an excellent stimulus to imagining just what this route would have been like in 1804. For a shorter and a bit more action packed introduction to the corps, see the National Geographic video, 1804-06 Lewis and Clark Expedition Documentary, available on YouTube.

Why Lewis and Clark?

Meriwether Lewis was Thomas Jefferson's secretary when Jefferson, and his fellow members of the American Philosophical Society, was looking for someone to lead the expedition to explore the newly acquired Louisiana Territory. Jefferson tasked Lewis with leading the expedition from recruiting members to purchasing materials. Lewis recruited William Clark who had once been his commander in the army, and the two of them put together the necessary provisions and crew for their westward journey.

Louisiana Territory: if you don't remember your history lesson, the Louisiana Territory stretched from the Mississippi River to the Rocky Mountains and included all the land in-between except for Texas and Eastern New Mexico. It doubled the size of the United States and was largely unknown territory to Anglo-Americans at that time. The purchase included 800,000 square miles of land and cost 23 million dollars.

His appointment of Lewis turned out to be a good choice. It's hard to imagine a better outcome then the one that resulted. Lewis and Clark returned with a wealth of information, and only one person died on the over 2-year exploration of largely unchartered territory (at least for the Europeans). Sadly, Lewis only lived three more years after the expedition's completion. Most researchers agree that Lewis committed suicide after some kind of mental breakdown in 1809. However, controversy continues to rage. A good, neutral source for the debate can be found here.

Jefferson tasked the men not only with finding a navigable water route that would connect the east to the West Coast, but with a myriad of other goals as well ranging from making friends and trading partners with the Indian tribes, mapping the territory, taking a flora, fauna, and natural resources inventory and discovering avenues for commerce (See Jefferson's letter here).

It's hard to appreciate today just how prescient Jefferson was in supporting such an expedition. If you are lucky enough to travel and explore parts of their journey, it is apparent just how spectacular this area was and is in natural beauty and resources. We may challenge the right of the Americans to claim this land as their own given that it was already largely populated, but it's hard not to appreciate the opportunity we have today to visit and explore such an amazing, and often pristine even today, landscape.

They departed on their exploration in May, 1804 from Wood River Illinois, and it took them 15 months to reach the headwaters of the Missouri River. They followed maps provided by other explorers, talked to the Native Americans along the route and looked for trails already blazed, but largely they followed the Missouri whenever possible. And, when the Missouri ran out, they chose rivers that seemed most likely to lead to the Pacific. They entered the Lemhi Valley in Idaho in August, 1805. Their total miles reached 3700, one way. And as we retrace parts or even all of that trip, we are lucky that so much of their journey traveled through beautiful and interesting places, many of which are largely unspoiled even today.

The Major Players

York was Clark's slave, but he participated fully in the expedition. He was given his freedom a few years after the expedition. This is probably the most thorough, brief, examination of York.

Toussaint Charbonneau, the Frenchman hired as a cook and interpreter for the corps, had two wives: one of which, Sacagawea, was chosen to accompany him on the journey.

Sacagawea, a young Shoshone woman who had been kidnapped five years previously by the Hidatsa, was selected to accompany the group because of her potential language skills if they were to encounter Native Americans and because traveling with a young woman and a child would make it clear the group was not a war-party. She helped the corps with directions, translations, and she helped them to buy needed horses.

Many of us know Sacagawea by her more "popular" name of Sacajawea, a Lemi Shoshone word meaning "boat pusher". Ironically, Sacajawea was the name given to her by a fictionalized account written years after the expedition. In the journals, Lewis and Clark always referred to her as Sacagawea (and variant spellings of this), a Hidatsa word meaning bird woman. (See Anderson, I. W. and Blanche Schroer, "Sacagawea. Her Name and Her Destiny." *We Continued On*. Nov. 1999, 6-9.)

George Drouillard had an extensive knowledge of the river, was a good hunter and knew Shawnee, French and Plains Indian Sign Language.

26 Enlisted men with a variety of useful skills including a few who spoke different Indian languages including Omaha and Hidatsa, others who knew carpentry and a couple of blacksmiths and gunsmiths.

Accuracy

This guide focuses on places that interpret the Lewis and Clark expedition as well as places where the corps stopped or passed through. Clark took regular "celestial" readings to provide location information and to map the territory they were exploring. However, there are times when this information was less than accurate. Some of the places included in here are still up for debate as the actual stop Lewis and Clark made. These are noted in the entry.

And, a note on Lewis and Clark's spelling. Lewis and Clark are notoriously creative spellers. The same word might be spelled in many different ways. This can be confusing for modern readers but, at the same time, captures their distinct voices. In most cases, I've used the actual journal spellings unless the variants create confusion.

Celestial Readings

Lewis and Clark were tasked by Jefferson with documenting the physical location of all important points they traversed. They took Celestial readings to provide the latitude and longitude. Clark drew extensive maps during the journey and worked on these maps for two years after the journey ended. Clark had some cartography experience from the Virginia frontier and in the Army. Lewis studied under Andrew Ellicott, the foremost surveyor of the day. During the expedition, they used a sextant to measure between the horizon and stars or planets to determine both latitude and longitude, but such readings depended on weather and the ability to spot the stars or planets. Longitude required a chronometer that had to be wound daily and/or celestial observations that required three assistants and could take the entire evening. Longitude gave Lewis trouble throughout the expedition, though latitude was easier to determine. Latitude is determined by measuring the angle of the moon and a star with an octant. They also used a telescope, compasses, a "Hadley's quadrant" and drafting instruments. Jefferson was responsible for teaching Lewis most of his celestial reading training. Because of the unreliability of the celestial readings and some inconsistency in keeping a journal, particularly on Lewis' part, it was not always possible to determine just where the corps stopped. Add to that all the major dams that have been added since 1806 (at least 6 on the Missouri, 15 on the snake, and 14 on the Columbia) and all the changes in river flows, and it becomes clearer why often a location is "in this area" rather than "right here."

Using this Guide

Travelers hoping to visit Lewis and Clark sites will have different ideas in mind for the journey: some may want only the "major" sites that focus almost exclusively on Lewis and Clark, others may want to combine major with more minor sites, and still others may wish to stop at every Lewis and Clark plaque on the road, minor and major site, in their destination area. In addition, while traveling through the area, most visitors also want to eat, sleep and maybe visit other worthy destinations. To try to meet the needs of most travelers, I've designed this book to include almost all Lewis and Clark sites, but they are marked as

📍 for Major,

📖 for minor and

📌 for other,

meaning a site worth visiting in the area, but not related to Lewis and Clark. As far as lodging and dining go, I've indicated interesting possibilities throughout the guide, but the focus in this guide is on the Lewis and Clark sites not on dining and lodging. And for those who would like to enrich their travel with some educational value, check out the resources section below and the info boxes throughout that provide general knowledge and educational resources about the Corps of Discovery.

Directions

Today, most of use some kind of electronic mapping to provide our directions. Wherever possible, I've provided addresses that can be used in electronic mapping. But paper maps are always a good idea especially if you plan on venturing into the backroads where your GPS may not work well. I love maps and use them almost exclusively, so I've also included general directions within each entry just in case you are not relying on your electronics. I've freely utilized abbreviations for North (N), South (S), East (E) and West (W) and for Interstates (I), state roads which will be abbreviated with a given state's abbreviation (SD for South Dakota, for example), Federal highways are abbreviated with US and then the number, and forest roads are FR and the number. If a road has a name and a number, I've tried to include both.

Bikers

The more adventurous may want to tackle some or all of the route by bike. *Adventure Cyclist* magazine has done much of the planning work for you. Check out their information at the website. The original plans for this route were made around 2004 during the bicentennial, but there are regular map updates added. Be sure to check those out.

On the River

Lewis and Clark did most of their trip on the water. It's certainly not necessary to be on the water to explore their route, but you may want to do some part of the trip on the river. Riverboats offer a variety of options for 3-7 day trips. But day-trips can also be done to enjoy the river experience.

American Queen Steamboat Company offers Lewis and Clark Cruises

Lewis and Clark Trail Adventures offers canoe trips on the Missouri

National Geographic offers Lewis and Clark Tours

ROW Adventures provides canoe trips from Great Falls that tour the Lewis and Clark trail on water.

Traveling with Children

This is a great trip to do with kids. Most interpretive and visitor centers have kid-geared activities, and children can work on earning their Lewis and Clark Junior Ranger badge, just ask at any national park or monument on your route. A wide variety of books on the expedition from fiction to non-fiction to activity books are available at the visitor centers. On frequent trips with my two children, the kids selected a book or activity at each visitor center. These helped fill the time in the car but also encouraged them to learn about the areas we were visiting.

Kids and teens might also enjoy a journal. This can be a traditional written notebook (be sure to encourage art work as well) just like Lewis and Clark's or they can keep a journal online. Check out this website for a selection of online journals https://www.commonsensemedia.org/lists/journal-apps-online. Encouraging kids to add pictures they take and their own drawings is an excellent way to keep them engaged.

Kids (and adults!) might enjoy this printable Lewis and Clark map to follow their own journey.

Create a scavenger hunt for the trip. You could use the Lewis and Clark list or make your own. See the glossary list in the Appendix 1 Scavenger Hunt for ideas. Kids can check items off the list as they locate them on the trip or take pictures to add to the scavenger hunt, building their own artifact list. Give small rewards when a certain number of items have been located.

Finally, look at the websites (listed throughout the guide) for the places you plan to stop and see what they have planned for children when you are visiting. If you are going in the summer, chances are there are specific children-themed activities you'll be able to take advantage of.

Resources for children

This video is a good introduction for the 6-12 crowd.

There are a large variety of nature journals on Amazon or in a local bookstore. Take your child with you and help them pick out one that appeals to their interests. Some include field guide identifications, places to keep pictures or brochures, sketch pads, and writing ideas.

Excellent bookstore along the trail (and also online):

Fort Clatsop Bookstore

Books for preschool and kindergarten

Lewis and Clark—A Prairie Dog for the President, Shirley Rose Redmond, 2003

I am Sacagawea, Brad Meltzer, 2017

A Picture Book of Sacagawea, David A Adler, 2001

A Picture Book of Lewis and Clark, David A Adler, 2003

The Lewis and Clark Expedition, John Perritano, 2010

Books for 2nd-6th

I am Sacajawea, I am York, Claire Rudolf Murphy and Higgins Bond, 2005

How We Crossed the West: The Adventured of Lewis and Clark, Rosalyn Schanzer, 2002

Lewis and Clark for Kids: Their Journey of Discovery with 21 Activities, Janis Herbert, 2000

Animals on the Trail with Lewis and Clark by Dorothy Hinshaw Patent, 2002

Dog of Discovery: A Newfoundland's Adventures with L&C, Laurence Pringle, 2004

Going Along with Lewis & Clark, Barbara Filter, 2000, this is one of my favorites for this age group. There are a lot of visuals with brief, useful descriptions.

I am #1 Sacagawea, Grace Norwich, 2012

Books for teens

York's Adventures with Lewis & Clark, Rhoda Blumberg, 2004

The Journal of Augustus Pelletier, Kathryn Lasky, 2000. This is a fictionalized account of a 14-year-old who goes along with the expedition. While fictionalized, it is a fun read.

Streams to the River, River to the Sea, Scott O'Dell, 2008

Lewis and Clark, A Museum in a Book, Rod Gragg, 2003 (I loved this book! It's great to take a long on the trip and includes many actual artifacts).

Sacajawea, Joseph Bruchac, 2008

When to Go

Most of the major sites can be accessed year-round from well-maintained roads. But if you want to take in some of the more remote destinations, travel is best from mid-May-mid-Oct, depending on snowfall. Some sites are seasonal as well and tend to be open from May through Sept. The end of May through the beginning of June is a great time to go. Temps are still fairly moderate with occasional rain. It's a good idea to bring along layers and a rain coat because weather can be unpredictable and can change quickly. Expect rain the closer you get to the Pacific!

Resources

The web has a wide range of Lewis and Clark resources. Many of these are from the 2004-2006 bicentennial celebration, so they may be somewhat dated in their visitor information, but the historic information is still accurate. I've selected some of the best to include here.

The largest collection of Lewis and Clark artifacts is at the Peabody Museum at Harvard.

Online

North Dakota State Historical Society Lewis and Clark Online Exhibit

Discovering Lewis and Clark, incredibly detailed look at the expedition from beginning to end.

National Park Lewis & Clark Trail Information

Maps

A variety of maps illustrating many of the routes is available at the Journals of the Lewis & Clark expedition.

Flora and Fauna

Plants Lewis and Clark Collected in Montana

Lewis and Clark's Scientific Discoveries: Plants: A guide to some of the plants that Lewis and Clark "discovered." While this guide is in no way comprehensive, it's easy to use and provides beautiful pictures of the plants.

Lewis & Clark as Naturalists, the Smithsonian has an online exhibit that includes specimens found by Lewis and Clark, where they were found and when. These are not the actual specimens that the corps sent East, but it's an excellent introduction to the flora and fauna.

Plants on the Trail with Lewis and Clark, Dorothy Hinshaw Patent, 2003

Primary Texts

The Lewis and Clark Journal Collection edited by respected scholar and Lewis and Clark expert, Gary Moulton at the University of Nebraska.

Native American Perspectives and Effects

Lewis & Clark Trail Tribal Legacy Project

Lifelong Learning Online: The Lewis and Clark Rediscovery Project, focuses on three tribes that encountered Lewis and Clark, Nez Perce, Warm Springs, and Coeur d'Alene. The site was created for the bicentennial, so it is dated, but the information is generally about the expedition so time doesn't really effect it's quality. Make sure to click through the tribe's name to get to the content. There's a lot of stuff here.

Trailtribes.org focuses on the tribes Lewis and Clark encountered not covered in Lifelong Learning Online.

Narrative Interpretations

Out West: A Journey Through Lewis & Clark's America, Dayton Duncan

Undaunted Courage, Stephen Ambrose

Artifacts and Tools

The Library of Congress has an excellent online library of Lewis and Clark items including letters from Jefferson and pictures of the items brought on the trip.

What to watch

PBS Documentary *Lewis & Clark-The Journey of the Corps of Discovery*

Companion Site to The Journey of the Corps of Discovery

Lewis and Clark-Great Journey West

A note on sources

This is not a scholarly work, but wherever possible reliable sources have been used including the Journals themselves, Lewis and Clark exhibits, the well-known and respected research journal, We Proceeded On, and a variety of scholarly books. In most cases, I have also visited the places included here, many on guided interpretive tours.

South Dakota

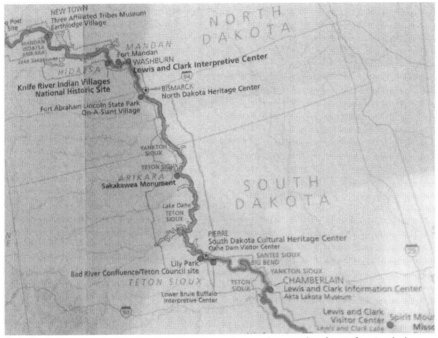

(South Dakota and North Dakota Map from the National Park Service)

The corps entered South Dakota at the SE tip in August 1804 and followed the boundary of South Dakota and Nebraska along the Missouri River until the river heads N into South Dakota at Pickstown. Their first order of business was to meet with the Omaha tribe, an event that never took place. Instead, they met with the Otoes and Missouris. When Lewis and Clark navigated the river in this area, it was often shallow and filled with sandbars over which the men had to tow their boats.

South Dakota Lewis and Clark Brochure

Further Exploration: Lewis and Clark encountered nearly 50 different Native American Tribes. PBS describes many of these tribes with which the corps had the most significant interactions.

Sioux City

I 29 enters South Dakota at Sioux City. The Missouri rivers runs along the S border of the city and is the dividing line between Nebraska and South Dakota. Nestled at the border of South Dakota, Iowa and Nebraska, North Sioux City is just across the border from Iowa. For the purposes of this guide, I've included destinations in the area regardless of which of the three states they are in.

Lewis and Clark spent several weeks in this area when Sergeant Floyd became ill on July 31, 1804. When the corps arrived, the area was almost devoid of Anglo-Americans with the exception of some French fur trappers and Spanish soldiers and bureaucrats.

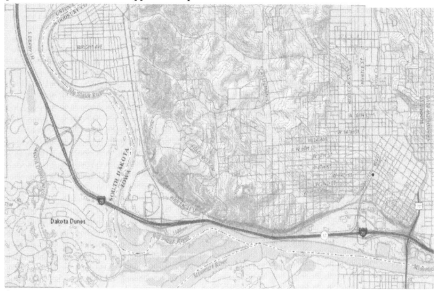

(USGS map)

🏛 **Adams Homestead Nature Preserve**, 272 Westshore Dr, exit 4 off I29 and go W on Northshore Dr (SD 23), 605-232-0873, https://gfp.sd.gov/parks/detail/adams-homestead-and-nature-preserve/, 6am-11pm park, 8am-4:30pm visitor center, restrooms, picnic shelter, 7 miles of hiking and biking trails, playground. Map.

1500 acre wooded preserve along the Missouri River and South Dakota and Nebraska border that includes restored historical buildings from 1872 including a church and school.

You can view one of the last free-flowing segments of the Missouri River that almost looks like Lewis and Clark saw it. If the river is low, you'll see sandbars that the corps would have had to navigate over. Visitors center includes exhibits on Lewis and Clark.

- **Dorothy Pecaut Nature Center**, 4500 Sioux River Rd, IA 12, 712-258-0838, http://woodburyparks.org/dorothy-pecaut-nature-center/, 9am-4:30 Tues-Sat, 1-4:30 Sun, closed Mon. trails, exhibits with live reptiles, fish and raptors, bird-viewing area, butterfly and wildflower gardens. Map.

- **Lewis and Clark Interpretive Center and Betty Strong Encounter Center**, 900 Larsen Park Rd, exit 149 off I-29, 712-224-5252, http://www.siouxcitylcic.com/, 9am-5pm, Noon-5pm Sat-Sun, closed Mon, free, picnic tables. Exploration Weds for kids in summer.

The interpretive center includes an exhibit on Sergeant Floyd, the only soldier to die on the expedition, and another exhibit on the expedition's passing through the area from July-Sept 1804. The exhibits also include what happened when a soldier deserted the expedition. Moses Reed deserted and was caught a few days later. His punishment was to run a gauntlet and receive 500 whip lashes. He was eventually discharged and did not complete the expedition.

The Encounter center exhibits focus on the meetings between the whites and the Native people. Lakota and Art exhibits are also on display. Many of the exhibits are interactive and make this a rewarding stop for visitors of all ages. Several outdoor sculptures of the corps including a 14ft bronze, "Spirit of Discovery" of Lewis, Clark and Seaman.

- **Sergeant Floyd River Museum**, 1000 Larsen Park Rd, 712-279-0198, http://www.siouxcitymuseum.org/sgt-floyd-river-museum-a-welcome-center, 10-4 daily, closed Major Holidays, free, restrooms, picnic shelter, playground, riverfront walking trail

Housed aboard the dry-docked M. V. Sergeant Floyd, this welcome center and museum provides local information and Missouri River history. An exhibit on Sergeant Floyd provides a life-size re-creation.

- **Sergeant Floyd Monument**, 2601 S Lewis Blvd, US 75, one mile N of I29 at exit 143, 202-354-2211, picnic tables, park.

  100 foot obelisk marks the final resting place of the only member of the Corps to die during the expedition. On August 20, 1804, Floyd died of what has since been diagnosed as a burst appendix. He was buried here in 1901 after two previous burials deteriorated and exposed the grave.

- **Sioux City Museum**, 607 4ᵗʰ St at Nebraska, 712-279-6174, http://www.siouxcitymuseum.org/sioux-city-public-museum, 10-5, Sun 1-5, closed Mon. Free.

  Local history including Native Americans and a hands-on archaeological dig. The museum includes multi-media presentations on Sioux City disasters and a computer generated interactive timeline. It's a very contemporary and engaging museum.

Take a break in downtown Sioux City at the **Schweddy's Hot Dog Shop** (211 4ᵗʰ St, 712-560-1370) for a Coney or pulled pork hot dog. Dogs are all beef and buns are from a local bakery.

Elk Point

Just up the road from Sioux City on I29 at exit 15, Elk Point is on the E side of the interstate, the Missouri River, along which Lewis and Clark were traveling, on the W side.

- **Heritage Park/Elk Point Park and Elk Point marker**, 400-498 S Harrison St, exit 18 off I29, 605-356-2141, camping, restrooms, picnic tables, playground.

  Lewis and Clark camped near here August 22, 1804 after the one and only corps member passed away S of here in the Sioux City area. Clark noted the numerous elk in in his journal. Some have called the replacement of the recently deceased Sgt Floyd the first election west of the Mississippi, but others state that while Lewis and Clark polled the group on who would replace Floyd, ultimately the decision lay with the leaders. This was a military expedition, after all, not a democratic corps. Patrick Gass was given the commission.

Take a break at **Ollies Drive Inn** (411 E Rose St, 605-356-2401). It has a huge menu of classic drive in foods. The soft serve ice cream is good, pork tenderloin is a classic but lots of other choices from pizza to burgers.

Vermillion

Continuing N and W along the Missouri, Vermillion is about 8m up the road from Elk Point on SD 50. Vermillion is a small college town that is home of University of South Dakota. Lewis and Clark camped at the mouth of the Vermillion River before trekking to Spirit Mound on August 25, 1804. Joseph Field killed the corps' first buffalo.

♀ **Spirit Mound Historic Prairie State Park**, 31148 SD 19, 6m N of Vermillion, 605-987-2263, https://gfp.sd.gov/parks/detail/spirit-mound-historic-prairie/ . Interpretive sign about Seaman, .75m hiking trail, restrooms, picnic tables. Open year round. Spirit Mound Learning and Information Center includes interactive computer terminals. Open daily except major holidays. Map. Field Guide.

Lewis, Clark, several of their men and Seaman walked nine miles from their camp to the mound to explore its composition on August 25, 1804. Apparently, Indians in the area feared the mound believing it was the residence of devils. Lewis and Clark hypothesized that the mound was geologic, and they were correct. It's a result of glacier movement, and its core is made of Niobrara chalk. Until recently, the mound was a cattle feedlot. In 1986 it was placed in the Spirit Mound Trust, and the city and University restored it to its original prairie ecosystem.

If you visit the mound on a hot day, you will appreciate how the corps felt when they visited. It was so hot that Seaman collapsed. Once they reached the top of the mound, they were rewarded by a beautiful view. It's worth a hike up the hill just to share the experience of Lewis and Clark and to see their views, but I wouldn't recommend it in August!

✦ **W.H. Over Museum**, 1110 University St, 605-659-6151, http://www.whovermuseum.org/, 10-4pm, closed on Sun.

W. H. Over was a naturalist of the northern plains from 1913-1945. Wide ranging collection of South Dakota natural and cultural history. Native American exhibits and historic photographs.

- **Clay County Park**, 460th Ave, 4m SW of Vermillion take SD 50 to Hwy.19 S to Timber Rd W to 460th Ave S, 605-624-5571, camping, picnic shelters, playground, 3.5m nature trail, boat ramp, fishing, restrooms

   34-acre park with spectacular views over the Missouri River. Last natural stretch of the Missouri.

- **Old Main/Oscar Howe Gallery**, Center of the USD campus (Map), 605-677-3177, 1-5, closed Sun.

   Gallery features the largest collection of American Indian artist Oscar Howe.

- **National Music Museum**, 414 E Clark St, 605-677-5306, www.nmmusd.org, 9-5, 2-5 Sun.

   Huge music museum including instruments from all over the world.

- **Missouri River and Mulberry Bend Overlook**, SD 19 S from Vermillion where you'll cross into NE to NE 15, restrooms. The overlook is on the E side of the highway, interpretive panels on hydrology, Native Americans and a devastating flood.

   While Lewis and Clark may not have traveled up here, it's not hard to imagine Lewis taking a look from this high point at the incredible, expansive views and the free-flowing Missouri. A short trail leads to the overlook and a longer trail winds to an upper viewpoint. Both are worth stopping for.

Take a break in this college town and you'll likely find yourself at a bar or pizza place. But there are a variety of chains at the E side of town on E Cherry St. off SD 50 or go S of Cherry St to Main for the campus area eats. **Café Brule** (24 W Main St, 605-624-2945, https://www.cafebrule.com/) is a good choice for all three meals with a mix of Mediterranean and comfort foods that will please almost anyone. They make a good Croque Monsieur Brule, but their meatloaf is tasty as well.

Yankton

Off SD 50, 23m N of Vermillion, Yankton sits right on the Missouri River on the SD and NE border. 4m west of Yankton is the dam and Lewis and Clark Visitor Center, in Nebraska, both on the Lewis and Clark lake.

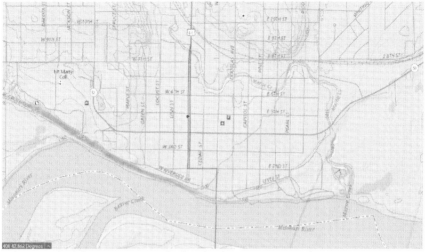

Dakota Territorial Museum, currently closed as it moves to a new site

🏛 **Lewis and Clark Visitor Center**, 55245 NE Hwy. 121, Crofton NE, drive S from Yankton on US 81, then W on NE 12 to NE 121 (2m S of the dam), 402-667-2546,

The visitor center stands on Calumet bluff where Lewis and Clark met with the Yankton Sioux in Aug 1804. Great views of the dam and the Missouri River. Lewis and Clark would have looked out over this bluff as well, but their view would have been significantly different. Exhibits and information displays on the development of the Missouri River including the Lewis and Clark expedition and native wildflowers. Take a walk through the Dorian Prairie Garden which includes interpretive panels.

Take a break in Yankton with pizza and wings at **Charlies** (804 Summit St, 605-665-2212). Some call this the best pizza in South Dakota. I haven't tried enough places to know if that's true, but the pizza is worth a stop. If you like your pizza saucy, ask for extra sauce.

📍 **Missouri National Recreational River**, 508 E 2nd St, 605-665-0209, https://www.nps.gov/mnrr/index.htm, camping, hiking, biking, trails, headquarters, 8-4:30 Mon-Fri, Map.

The headquarters building in Yankton is a great place to get information on the Missouri River and Lewis and Clark.

100 miles of river make up this recreation area, including two free flowing stretches of the Missouri. The river trail extends from Sioux City to Pickstown SD. There are two districts: the 39m district below Yankton, and the 59m district above Yankton. Touring either section of

the river with a canoe or kayak is probably one of the most realistic ways to experience the Lewis and Clark expedition. For detailed information on navigating the river and taking advantage of opportunities to explore the flora and fauna, check out the MNRR site. There is not an official visitor center, but the headquarters includes information about the park including junior ranger booklets. A mobile ranger station makes its way up and down the river area during the summer. Lewis and Clark camped on Aug 22-25 on the 59-mile segment stretching past Yankton.

- **Pierre Dorion Monument Lewis and Clark Site**, W Second and Riverside Dr.

   Pierre Dorion was the first white settler in the area and interpreted Lakota for the corps. His monument is here, near his gravesite.

- **Chief White Crane Recreation Area**, 31323 Toe Rd, 605-668-2985, $6 per vehicle, camping, cabins, bird watching, hiking trail, Map.

   Chief White Crane (Martoree) met with Lewis and Clark on Aug 30. The Corps spent the night with the Yankton and shared breakfast and a peace pipe the next day.

- **Pierson Ranch Recreation Area**, 31144 Toe Rd, off SD 52, 605-668-2985, camping, picnic shelters, playground, Map and guide.

- **Lewis and Clark Recreation Area**, 43349 SD 52, 6m W of Yankton, 605-668-2985, http://www.lewisandclarkpark.com/, $6 per day, restrooms, camping, cabins, resort, restaurant, boating, fishing, jet skiing, swimming, archery range, hiking trails
   Map.

- **Gavins Point Dam and Spillway**, Crest Rd, W of Yankton Hwy. 52 then S, 402-667-2546, http://www.nwo.usace.army.mil/Missions/Dam-and-Lake-Projects/Missouri-River-Dams/Gavins-Point/, Dam Mon-Fri 8-4pm March-Oct., camping, restrooms, playground.

   Interpretive displays for Lewis and Clark and for the Missouri National Recreational River. The archaeological record for this area dates back to between 3000-5000 BC. Video on Lewis and Clark. Tours of the dam are available.

★ **The Gavins Point National Fish Hatchery and Visitor Center**, 31227 436ᵗʰ Ave, 3m W on Hwy. 52 before the dam turn-off, 605-665-3352, 10-3 Mon-Fri April, Sept; May-Labor Day 10-5 daily. Nature trails. 10,000 gallons of display space.

The Sioux

The Sioux at the time Lewis and Clark were heading west were generally feared. And, Jefferson had specifically requested that Lewis and Clark make a good impression on the Sioux because of their strength and fearlessness. Their name "Sioux" comes from a French word for "Little Snakes". The Sioux had recently migrated to the plains and had become the most powerful tribe in the area. There were multiple tribes of Sioux that remained largely disparate even when fighting against the Army. In 1804, estimates of their population ranged about 12,000. Lewis and Clark encountered the Yankton Sioux in South Dakota, a tribe of about 1600-2000 people. They greeted the corps with friendship and eagerly traded, but Lewis and Clark noted their tendency to steal and their frequent battles with other tribes. Their interactions with the Sioux would vary from convivial dancing and eating to violent encounters. For the Lakota, the evidence of the "white men's" might was of less concern than the threat they represented for the Lakota trading system. This tension would create considerable difficulty each time they met. And the Sioux would continue to strike fear in both Natives and Whites through the 19ᵗʰ century culminating in their victory at the Battle of Little Bighorn in 1876. After that victory, however, the Lakota, the last of the Sioux still fighting, were finally quelled.

Springfield

Springfield at SD 37 is 35 miles W of Yankton and sits upon a bluff that overlooks the Missouri River. Here in September 1804, Lewis and Clark probably stood to take in the expansive views. Lewis and Clark spent the night on a nearby ravine and on one of the islands, Bon Homme, in the river, which is now under water.

★ **Springfield Recreation Area**, 1412 Boat Basin Drive, 605-668-2985, $6, camping, boating, cabins, golf, bike trail, Map.

Pickstown

SD 50 continues W moving away from the Missouri for about 70 miles and then enters Pickstown, just N of the Missouri on SD 46. Here, the corps first identified the prairie dog though they did not call it that. They went to great trouble to catch one of these, pouring five barrels of water down a hole to evict the dog and then capturing him. And, they were told by local Indians to keep an eye out for "burning bluffs" along the river as they traveled. The phenomena were a result of a chemical reaction in the shale.

Several recreation areas line the river in this area, all of which Lewis and Clark passed in late Sept, early Oct 1804. **Fort Randall Dam** (see below) provides the most services including interpretive panels on the expedition. Others include: **Indian Creek Recreation Area**, 12905 288ᵗʰ Ave, Mobridge, 605-845-7112; **North Point Recreation Area**, US18/281 to 38180 297ᵗʰ St; **Buryanek Recreation Area**, 27450 Buryanek Rd, 605-337-2587; **Lake Andes**, US 18 to 388ᵗʰ Ave N, 605-487-7046. Lake Andes is a separate body of water from the River.

⌂ **Karl E Mundt National Wildlife Refuge,** S of Pickstown, closed to public use.

In Sept 1804, the expedition camped near this area where they encountered bison, wolves and prairie dogs. Many of the species that Lewis and Clark viewed are still living in the area including bald eagles, red fox, western grebes.

⌂ **Fort Randall Dam and Francis Case Lake**, S of Pickstown on SD 46, 605-487-7845, visitor center (US 281 and 18, 8-5:30), restrooms, camping, fishing, hunting, boating, sailing, swimming, playground, interpretive signs, tours in summer. The remains of the fort are accessible at the dam. Map.

Today the grounds can be walked and the visitor center provides exhibits on Lewis and Clark. Also see interpretive signs on Target Hill overlook at the west end of the dam.

The area upon which the dam sits has been inhabited for at least 8000 years. The Mandan and Arikara arrived around 1750 AD, but they were pushed into North Dakota with the arrival of the Sioux who quickly adapted to plains living using the buffalo as food.

In late-August early Sept 1804, Lewis and Clark came through the area. On Sept. 10, Clark found the fossil remains of the backbone, teeth and ribs of some sea-dwelling creature. Two miles upriver from here, the corps camped on their return journey on Aug 30th, 1806 where Lewis threatened a group of Sioux with death if they approached the camp. Relations between the corps and the Lakota had deteriorated badly.

The Fort was built 50-years after the Lewis and Clark expedition in 1856.

Lake Francis Case drowned the corps' campsite. The lake sits behind the dam and covers just over 100 miles and has 540 miles of shoreline. Lake Andes and Karl E Mundt wildlife refuges on the lake protect a number of species.

Platte

Upriver from Pickstown, Platte is about 15m E of the Missouri at SD 44 and 45.

Take a break and spend the night in **Molly's Manor** (810 S Main Ave, 605-337-2294, http://www.mollysmanor.com/Home_Page.php), and enjoy a from scratch breakfast and stay in one of the bedrooms or larger suites decorated in casual country style with quilts and simple colors.

🏠 **Snake Creek**, 35316 SD 44, 14m W of Platte, 605-337-2587, $6, camping, cabins, picnic areas, hiking, biking, boating, fishing, restaurant, Map.

Snake Creek sits on Lake Francis Case and includes day use and camping areas. Views over the Missouri from the recreation area.

Read the interpretive panel that explains how the youngest of the expedition managed to get lost on Sept 11, 1804 and, luckily, found. Private George Shannon had gone out to locate some run-away horses and was unable to relocate the corps. It was two weeks later as Shannon was literally starving that he finally found them downstream from him. Lewis and Clark identified the sharp-tailed grouse here on Sept. 12, which they attempted to send home to Jefferson. Sadly, the grouse did not survive the trip.

Specimens Go East

Lewis and Clark sent their specimens home from Fort Mandan at the end of March, 1805 in the large keelboat and with a small detachment of men. The specimens included maps, reports of tribes, nature, geology, trading and culture. In addition, they included many specimens of soil, minerals, plants and even animals. The boat had to travel down the Missouri and Mississippi, through New Orleans and then by ship around Florida and back up the coast to Washington. The package finally arrived, a bit worse for wear, but surprisingly intact on August 12, 1805. And while several of the live animals died, a few made it to Jefferson.

Chamberlain

Chamberlain sits on the E side of the Missouri on I90. Oacoma is on the W side of the river. SD 50 is Main st and goes N up the river.

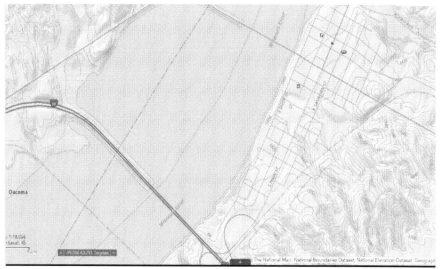

In this area, Lewis and Clark identify their first pronghorn on Sept. 14, 1804, calling it a "goat". They also identified several other species here including the jackrabbit, mule deer and the magpie, which they also sent home. One of the four they packed off actually survived the trip.

🛖 **Lewis and Clark Interpretive Center/Chamberlain Information Center**, I 90, exit 264 (look for the rest area), 605-734-4562, 8am-5pm, seasonal, free.

You'll see the "teepee" poles from the freeway. Views of Lake Francis Case from the keelboat shaped balcony. Exhibits depict the items the explorers brought on their journey and the wildlife they encountered. Climb aboard the 55-ft keelboat and check out the supplies Lewis and Clark would have packed with them. Murals depict the expedition. The center is located near the campsite from Sept 16–18, 1804 when the expedition stopped to dry out their provisions after steady rain for three days. The Dignity statue was installed in 2016.

✦ **Roam Free Park**, SD 50 N of Chamberlain, vault toilets, sheltered picnic tables, nature trails and native grasslands with views over the Missouri.

Take a break for some traditional South Dakota food at **Al's Oasis** (1000 East SD 16, 605-234-6054) in Oacoma (across the river) for classic "Chislic", a kebab style meat. But don't hesitate to try the Indian taco or one of their buffalo burgers. It can be a busy place, so if it looks crowded, head over to the **Butter Churn Bistro & Creamery** (103 N Main, 605-234-0196) back on the Chamberlain side, for house made fresh sandwiches with specials that vary day by day. See their facebook page for their specials.

🏛 **Akta Lakota Museum and Cultural Center at St. Joseph's Indian School**, 1301 North Main St, exit 263 off I90 and 2m North, 800-798-3452. http://aktalakota.stjo.org/, 8am-6pm May-Oct, 8-4 Nov-Apr, closed weekends, free.

Sioux history, heritage and culture. "Akta Lakota" means "to honor the people."

Exhibits are arranged to reflect the four cardinal directions and colors and follow a chronological structure starting with the pre Euro-American contact, to the meetings of the Lakota with Euro-Americans, to the broken promises of the US government and finally to how the Lakota are currently adapting. Be sure to go outside and check out the Medicine Wheel Garden. It's a beautiful and peaceful place.

The Two Worlds Meet exhibit focuses on the Sioux meetings with Lewis and Clark. On Sept 23, 1804, three young native boys tell Lewis and Clark that their chiefs are camped at the next creek. Lewis and Clark indicate they would like to meet with them.

Fort Thompson

Up SD 50 from Chamberlain, on SD 34/47, Fort Thompson sits on the E side of the Missouri. Fort Thompson and nearby Brule were relocated to their current sites when their original location was inundated by Big Bend dam in the 1960's.

🏛 **Lake Sharpe/Big Bend Dam**, SW on SD 47, 605-245-2255, camping, fishing, boating, playground, picnic areas

Lake Sharpe flows from the Oahe Dam upriver to Big Bend at Fort Thomspon covering 56,000 acres and 200 miles of shoreline. The Big Bend is created by a 25-mile circular curve just north of the dam. The thin strip of land just 1.5m between the two ends of the bend is known as "the narrows".

Left Trailrace area is located below the dam and provides full facilities.

Clark walked the narrows and noted ample wildlife as they passed through in Late Sept 1804. They also saw many Arikara and Sioux encampments. The wildlife is still abundant including Canadian Geese, duck, antelope and a variety of fish. The bison once thrived here on buffalo grass and grama (a type of dense grass). Drive the Native American Scenic Byway for a close-up scenic look along the river bluffs and high plains.

The Corps had quite an adventurous night here, writing

"Between one and two o'clock the sergeant on guard alarmed us, by crying that the sandbar on which we lay was sinking. We jumped up, and found that both above and below our camp the sand was undermined and falling in very fast. We had scarcely got into the boats and pushed off, when the bank under which they had been lying fell in, and would certainly have sunk the two periogues (canoes) if they had remained there. By the time we reached the opposite shore the ground of our encampment sunk also. We formed a second camp for the rest of the night, and at daylight proceeded on to the gorge or throat of the Great Bend, where we breakfasted. A man, whom we had despatched to step off the distance across the bend, made it 2000 yards; the circuit is 30 miles. During the whole course, the land of the bend (north of the Missouri) is low, with occasional bluffs; that on the opposite side, high prairie ground and long ridges of dark bluffs."

🏕 **West Bend State Recreation Area**, 22154 West Bend Rd, 605-773-2885, SD 34, $6, camping, cabins, fishing, hunting, bird watching, boating, Map.

Lewis and Clark campsite for Sept 20, 1804 is nearby.

The Missouri makes a big loop that almost creates a full circle and Clark reported that the area between the ends of the loop was 2000 yards while the area on the water was 30 miles.

Fort Pierre

Fort Pierre, at the intersection of US 83 and 14, is right across the Missouri River from Pierre. US 14 bridges the cities. Fort Pierre is the oldest white settlement in the state. Native Americans settled, traded and passed through the area frequently in the 18th and 19th century. Today, Fort Pierre is undergoing significant change and development as new housing is built and a marina is coming in.

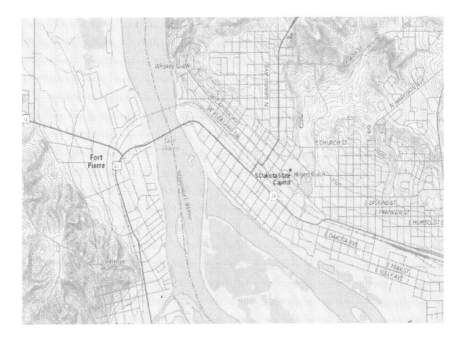

🏛 **Lewis and Clark Bicentennial Trail**, 30 miles of trails between Pierre and Fort Pierre which wind through urban and woodlands, prairies and waterfront. Maps of trails.

♀ **Fischers Lilly Park/Bad River Encounter Site**, 411 Ash Ave, 1st st SW of the river branch to E Cedar Abe to Casey Tibbs St N to Ash Ave., 605-223-7690, restrooms, interpretive panels, foot bridge across the river is accessible from the side of the Fort Pierre Swimming Pool

E Across the river, on what is now La Framboise Island, on Sept 25 1804, the corps met with three Teton Sioux chiefs. After a meeting and a tour of their keelboat, Clark returned the Teton chiefs to the shore only to be detained by three of the Sioux warriors. What might have turned into a fight was defused by the Teton Chief Black Buffalo. The man referred to the island as "Bad Humor' island because of the encounter. Clark wrote,

" *raised a Flag Staff & made a orning or shade on a Sand bar in the mouth of Teton River, for the purpose of Speeking with the Indians… we feel much at loss for the want of an interpreter the one we have can Speek but little … met in Council … envited those Cheifs on board to Show them our boat; soon began to be troublesom... Proceeded on about 1 mile & anchored out off a Willow Island, I call this Island bad humered Island as we were in a bad humer".*

✦ **La Framboise Island**, 28563 Powerhouse Rd, W. Sioux Ave to Poplar Ave SW to the island, foot traffic only on island, 605-224-5862, biking, fishing, picnic shelter, 8m nature loop, interpretive sign is on the River Trail on the W side of the island. Map. See listing under Fischers Lilly Park above.

✦ **Verendrye Museum,** Deadwood St, 605-223-7690, 9-4pm, 11-4 Sun, call for hours in the off season, named after two French explorer brothers, the museum features wild west history and pioneer days

✦ **The Casey Tibbs Rodeo Center**, 210 Verendrye Dr, 605-494-1094, http://www.caseytibbs.com/, 9-5, 1-5 Sun, closed Sun and Mon Sept-May, $6 adults, $4 children.
   Rodeo memorabilia and exhibits

✦ **Oahe Downstream Recreation Area**, 20439 Marina Loop Rd, 6m N of Fort Pierre on SD 1806, 602-223-7722, https://gfp.sd.gov/parks/detail/oahe-downstream-recreation-area/, $6, camping, archery, biking, birdwatching, fishing, demonstrations and events, butterfly garden, Map.
   231 miles of reservoirs that connect Pierre SD to Bismarck ND. Bald eagles are often seen here. The recreation area spreads from the SW side of the Missouri at SD 1806, across SD 204 to the E side of the river and SD 1804. N on 1804 is East Shore Recreation Area and N is Tailrace Recreation Area.

✦ **Oahe Dam Visitor Center**, 28563 Powerhouse Rd, 8m N off SR 1804 from Pierre and off 1806 off Fort Pierre on the Missouri River, 605-224-5862, 9-4pm visitor center, call for tour information, history of the lake and exhibits on construction and power generation.

✦ **Spring Creek Recreation Area**, 20439 Marina Loop Rd, 15m NW of Pierre off SD 1804 to SD 805 W, 605-223-7722, $6, vault toilets, fishing, hiking, full service resort (see below).

✦ Take a break: Looking for a good meal in this area, try the **Spring Creek Restaurant** in the **Spring Creek Resort** (28229 Spring Creek Place,

Pierre, 605-224-8336, opens May 1, all meals, http://www.springcreeksd.com/) with steak and fish as highlights

Pierre

Just across the river from Fort Pierre, Pierre is the Capitol of South Dakota and sits at US 14 and SD 34.

Take a break in Pierre at one of many restaurant choices along W. Sioux Ave downtown (SD 34).

- **Farm Island State Recreation Area and Lewis and Clark Visitor Center**, 1301 Farm Island Rd, 4m E of Pierre, 605-773-2885, $6, visitor center, archery, biking, birdwatching, boating, camping, fishing, 8m hiking trails, Map.

  Lewis and Clark stopped on the island to hunt for elk on Sept 24, 1804. Interactive displays in the interpretive center. Great views from the campground.

- **South Dakota Cultural Heritage Center**, 900 Governors Dr, 605-773-3458, http://www.sdhsf.org/society/visit_video.html, 9-6:30 summer, 9-4:30 the rest of the year, $4, children are free.

  Focus is on Native American cultural heritage including many of the tribes that Lewis and Clark encountered including the Yankton and Teton Sioux and the Arikara. The site includes a full-size tipi and bullboat, and an original Jefferson peace and friendship medal. The three galleries include Native Peoples, explorers and current SD history. This is a good place to get an introduction to both South Dakota and Lewis and Clark.

- **Fort Pierre National Grassland**, US 83S of Pierre to W FS 227, ranger station is at 1020 N Deadwood (8-12, 1-5 M-F), 602-224-5517, fishing, bird watching, wildflowers.

  Mixed prairie spanning 116,000 acres.

Forest City

From Pierre, US 83 goes N, away from the Missouri, Forest City is W on US 212 but to get to the West Whitlock, go E, briefly on US 212 and then N on 83.

- **West Whitlock Recreation Area**, 16157 West Whitlock, 18m W of Gettysburg off US 212 to SD 1804 N, 605-765-9410, $6, camping, birdwatching, fishing, hiking. Map.

  Full-sized replica of an Arikara lodge like the one Lewis and Clark visited 200 years ago. The lodge is made of cottonwood logs, willow branches and grass and could house 20 people.

Mobridge

This town, on the Missouri on US12 about 60m N of Forest city, sits where Lewis and Clark camped Oct 8-10, 1804 and encountered their first Arikara village at the mouth of the Grand River. A smallpox epidemic had decimated the Arikara in 1780, perhaps killing 20,000 people.

Take a Break

In this part of the country, there are few options for a good meal. **Great Plains Family Restaurant** (122 W Grand Crossing, 605-845-7495) is a reliable comfort food choice. Fried chicken and a slice of fresh pie is a good choice.

Step back in time and take in the local **Drive In Theater** (1600 20th St, 605-845-2021) see what's showing here, http://pheasantdrivein.weebly.com/now-showing-and-coming-soon.html, open on weekends.

- **Sacagawea Monument**, Hwy. 12 w from Mobridge to SD 1806 S, follow signs to Sitting Bull's grave. The corps passed through in October 1804.

  This is a pillar erected in 1929 that describes Sacagawea's contributions to the expedition. This has to be one of the most strange Sacagawea monuments on the trail. One wonders why a pillar was selected. . .

- **Lewis and Clark Interpretive Trail**, accessible on the SW side of town from Park Blvd/Main St , Railroad St and 20th St W, 2m. Lewis and Clark interpretive panels.

- **The Scherr-Howe Event Center**, 212 Main St, Mon-Fri, free.

  Basketball court with Lewis and Clark Murals created by Oscar Howe for the WPA project in 1942. The murals were refurbished in 2014.

- **Klein Museum**, 1820 W Grand Crossing, 605-845-7243, http://www.mobridgekleinmuseum.com/, 9-12, 1-5 Mon-Fri, 1-4 Sat-Sun from May 1-Oct 15.

  Preserves the history and culture of the local area with a focus on Sitting Bull. Outdoor buildings include school, house, and post office. An Arikara earth lodge replica is also on site.

Kenel

Following SD 1806 N 27 m from Mobridge, you'll move away from the Missouri and then back towards it as you reach Kenel.

- **Fort Manuel**, Kenel, SD 1806, accessible on a dirt un-marked road, if you are coming from the S, the turn off is on the E side of 1806 before 1st St. Follow signs then a short walking trail.

This is where history suggests Sacagawea died of fever in 1812 at the age of 25. A historical marker explains this theory, a couple of interpretive panels describe Sacajawea, and there are several old buildings in the field, which are not the original fort but replicas built in the 1960's.

Pollock

Pollock is directly across the Missouri from Kenel. If you are in a boat, you can just cross the channel. If you are in a car, it's considerably longer. Head back S on SD 1806 to Mobridge and then back N on SD 1804 for a total of 62m.

    ☺   **Lewis and Clark historical markers**, SD 1804 and 249th Ave, tells the story of the Legend of Stone Idol Creek. This is a Creek legend told to Lewis and Clark on Oct 10th when the corps visited an Arikara village. And, a sign on the Arikara. Private John Newman was court martialed here as well.

North Dakota

The Corps reached Bismarck North Dakota on Oct. 26, 1804 and decided to winter at Fort Mandan near several Native American villages. They stayed here for five months as they completed their preparations for the long push west.

Fort Yates

Part of the Standing Rock Sioux Reservation, Fort Yates sits both on and in the Missouri River. Depending on the depth of the water, the area of land that connects the E and W side of the town is more or less under water. ND 24/1806 passes through the W side of the town. From Kenel, Fort Yates is directly N.

The Corps was here on Oct 15, 1804. When Lewis and Clark arrived, the Cheyenne inhabited an earth lodge village here. In 1863 the fort was built to oversee the Lakota. One of the buildings of the fort still remains.

Indian Wars

Lewis and Clark didn't just come upon Native Tribes living peacefully on the plains, they entered an area in the midst of upheaval and tribal warfare. French traders and fur trappers had already been through the area, often bringing disease with them, but also guns and/or the promise of guns. Small pox swept the tribes in the 1780's, temporarily slowing down their battles, but by the mid to late 1790's, the Sioux, Mandan, Hidatsa, Omaha, Arikara, Crow and perhaps others were battling with one another. The Yellowstone River Valley was a contested area between the Crow and Lakota. When Lewis and Clark arrived, Clark noted that the Omaha were attempting to establish peace with the Lakota, and the corps repeatedly tried to patch up relationships among different tribes. As we look back at the situation on the plains and in the mountains when Lewis and Clark arrived, it's easy to see simplistic order or to get confused by all the different groups involved. What did the natives think when this group arrived? Did they feel as if they were intruding into their territory? Were they bringing disease? Were they friendly?

- ✦ **Sitting Bull Visitor Center**, 9299 Hwy. 24, on Sitting Bull College Campus, 701-854-8000, 8-5 Mon-Fri.

- ☫ **Lewis and Clark Legacy Nature Trail**, Prairie Knight Marina on SD 1806 N of Fort Yates, picnic tables, restrooms, 3m walking/biking trail with nature interpretive signage. Good place to see some of the plants that Lewis and Clark may have viewed.

Mandan

Mandan is just across the Missouri river from Bismarck Off I94. From Fort Yates, continue to follow the Missouri N for 62m to Mandan.

- ☫ **Fort Abraham Lincoln State Park/On a Slant Village**, 4480 Ft. Lincoln Rd, 7m S of Mandan on Hwy. 1806, 701-667-6340. Tours available. Camping, visitor center, cabins, picnic areas, playground. Map.

  Fort brings together Native American and Lewis and Clark history. The Fort was once an infantry and cavalry post from which Custer set out for Little Big Horn. And before that it was the site of an ancient Mandan Village, On a Slant Village, which now hosts five reconstructed earthlodges overlooking the Heart and Missouri Rivers.

  Lewis and Clark came across the deserted villages in Oct. 1804. It is likely that a smallpox epidemic decimated the Mandan village in 1781. The Lewis and Clark overlook is a short hike to some interpretive panels where you can view the Missouri as Lewis and Clark might have. Below the overlook was also a major battle between the Sioux, Assiniboine and Mandan in 1803. The battle was won by the Yanktonai Sioux.

🏠 **Huff Indian Village**, I94 exit to ND 25 N to CR 139A E, to 25th St N, 7.5m from Mandan, 701-328-2666, http://history.nd.gov/historicsites/huff/index.html, Free. Interpretive signs throughout the site.

Classic prehistoric Mandan site dating to 1000-1450. But the site was abandoned when Lewis and Clark come through.

Bismarck

The capitol city of North Dakota, Bismarck sits on the E side of the Missouri River. I94 runs through the N side of the city. Bismarck is directly across the river from Mandan.

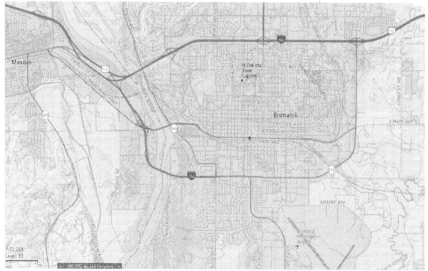

🏛 **Dakota Zoo**, 620 Riverside Park Rd, 701-223-7543, https://www.dakotazoo.org/, 10-7pm, $9.50, $6.50 children.

Thanks to the work of Kelly Heitkamp, a girl scout, the zoo has a guide to the Lewis and Clark animals. Heitkamp identified the animal that Lewis and Clark saw and includes quotes from the journal. Touring the zoo with this guide is a great way to introduce kids to the expedition.

★ **State Historical Society/North Dakota Heritage Center**, 612 East Boulevard Ave, 701-328-2666, https://statemuseum.nd.gov/, 8am-5pm Mon-Fri, 10-5 Sat-Sun., free. Café

Excellent history and culture museum. Well worth a visit. If you have the time, spend a half day here. It provides a good introduction to the native peoples that Lewis and Clark encounter, and it's a very contemporary, nicely curated museum.

🏛 **Sakakawea Statue**, 612 E Boulevard Ave, US Capitol National Statuary Hall

12ft high statue of Sakakawea and Pomp created by Leonard Crunelle. This spelling of Sakakawea is the accepted spelling in Bismarck.

🏛 **Keelboat Park**, 1605 River Rd, 701-222-6455, nontraditional park with some interesting sculptures including a keelboat, beautiful flowers and a view of the water. Maps.

🏛 **Double Ditch Indian Village**, on SD 1804, 7.5m N of Bismarck, 701-328-2666, http://www.history.nd.gov/historicsites/doubleditch/index.html, walking paths, interpretive signs

This once large earth lodge village is located high on a panoramic bluff and was inhabited by the Mandan Indians until 1785 for 300 years. When Lewis and Clark visited in Oct 1804, the area was already deserted probably as a consequence of smallpox. The site has recently undergone archaeological stabilization as severe erosion effects are repaired.

★ **North Dakota State Capitol**, 600 E Boulevard Ave, 701-328-2480, https://www.nd.gov/omb/public/state-capitol-information, 7:30-5 Mon-Fri, tours are offered daily.

★ **Lewis and Clark Riverboat**, 1700 N River Rd, 701-255-4233, https://www.lewisandclarkriverboat.com/, tour the Missouri River listening to a recorded city tour.

Hensler

N of Bismarck and Mandan, follow ND 25 N for 40 miles. Cross Ranch is just S of Hensler. On Aug 17, 1806, the corps camped near here and Clark paid Charbonneau his $500.33 salary. Charbonneau, Sacagawea and little Pomp departed from the group.

Cross Ranch Nature Preserve, 1401 River Rd, 7m S of Washburn, 701-794-8741, https://www.nature.org/ourinitiatives/regions/northamerica/unitedstat es/northdakota/placesweprotect/cross-ranch-preserve.xml, 2.3m nature trail, free, open dawn to dusk. Services are available across the street at Cross Ranch State park.

Here you have the opportunity to view the only free flowing section of the Missouri River and riparian cottonwood forests in North Dakota. This is a chance to see the river as Lewis and Clark may have seen it. It's a good place to view birds (90 species have been recorded), wildlife and the mixed-grass prairie of the 19th century. Wild bison herds may also be viewed. Located near both the outbound campsite of Oct 24, 1804 and the return site of Aug 17, 1806.

Washburn

Washburn is located on US 83 on the Missouri River. From Hensler, however, you will want to follow ND 200 for 9 miles. Fort Mandan is on the N side of the Missouri off SD 17 and the interpretive center is on 8th St SW.

McClean County Museum, 602 Main Ave, 701-462-3660, 10-4, 1-4 Sat, closed Sun, by appointment in the winter, free.

Lewis and Clark history and mural. The mural is on the outside wall of the building beside the original museum on Main st.

- **North Dakota Lewis and Clark Interpretive Center**, 2576 Eight St SW, Hwy. 83 and ND 200A, 701-462-8535, http://www.fortmandan.com/, 9-5pm closed Sundays in Winter, $8.

  Three life size statues of Lewis, Clark and Chief Sheheke greet visitors at the entrance. Emphasis is on the time the expedition spent at Fort Mandan during the winter of 1804-1805 including a reconstruction of Fort Mandan. Art and history of the area are also included. The Lewis and Clark gallery includes 100 items from the John Fisher collection that replicate items used on the expedition. A life-size exhibit features Clark writing in his journal. Enjoy sweeping views of the Missouri from the deck.

- **Washburn Discovery Trail**, intersection of ND 200 and US83 and accessible from the Interpretive Center, restrooms, interpretive signs, 2.2m hike

- **Fort Mandan**, 838 28th Ave SW, 2m S of the Big Hidatsa Village, 701-462-8535, http://www.fortmandan.com/default.asp, fortmandan.com, 9-5pm, $8 adult, $5 student.

  The Fort focuses on the Corps interactions with the local Native tribes in the winter of 1804-1805. The Corps constructed this village quickly in Oct 1804 hoping to beat the coming winter. While they were building, Lewis noted on Nov. 6th that the corps had viewed the Northern Lights. They quickly built two rows of huts of four rooms each using the local cottonwood trees, about 14 square feet. Around the fort, they built an 18ft stockade. The replica captures the size of their winter quarters, though it is difficult to imagine what living here over several months would be like. Temperatures reached 45 degrees below zero. They completed the fort in Dec.

  They selected this area because of how friendly the Mandan and Hidatsa were. The Corps hunkered down here for the winter months, talking with the locals, preparing for the next phase of their travels and sending off specimens to Jefferson in Washington. Sacagawea had her son on Feb. 11, 1805. They finally departed in April, 1805. They were now headed out to areas they had little to no knowledge of.

  Visitors can tour the fort and see inside the rooms which are arranged to look like the rooms from 1804.

The limits of knowledge

If you get to Fort Mandan, it's a great opportunity to imagine the interaction between these two such different cultures living within such close proximity of one another for several months. It was an excellent chance for Lewis and Clark to gather information that Jefferson had requested about the tribes and to learn about their culture, food, clothing and traditions. They shared everything, including the women. And both Lewis and Clark are believed to have fathered children with Native wives. But, it's also important to remember all the assumptions that Lewis and Clark would draw from what is actually only ¼ of a year with the Mandan. Traditions, ceremonies, clothing and food varied widely across the seasons, so Lewis and Clark were only getting one season's worth of experience. Drawing conclusions about the tribes from this ultimately brief if intimate interaction has led to many mistaken conclusions or erroneous beliefs about the Mandan. It is a reminder of how limited our knowledge is even when we can immerse ourselves with another people. A good starting point for understanding the cultural differences is within this Library of Congress online exhibition, *Rivers, Edens, Empires: Lewis and Clark and the Revealing of America.*

Stanton

Continuing on ND 200, which runs mostly along the Missouri here, for 22 miles to Stanton.

- **Knife River Indian Village NHS**, .5m N of Stanton ND on County Rd. 37. 701-745-3309, https://www.nps.gov/knri/index.htm. Visitor Center, 7:30-6 in summer, 8-4:30 in winter, hiking trails, exhibits.

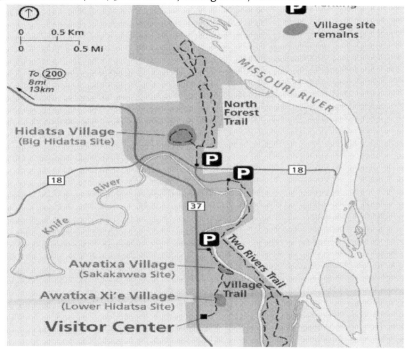

(Map is from the Knife River Village NHS website).

This almost 1800 acre site, preserves the historic and archaeological history of the Northern Plains Indians over an 8000 year time-span. Visitors can tour the museum with exhibits on the Hidatsa, walk through an earthlodge replica and visit Hidatsa gardens.

Lewis and Clark entered the area in Oct. in 1804. They encountered their first Native Americans on Oct 24th at the mouth of the Knife River. They were camping in nearby Fort Mandan. Big Hidatsa Village Site is part of the Indian Village NHS and was occupied when Lewis and Clark came through. The site included 120 circular earthlodges each of which probably housed around 25 people. At the time that Lewis and Clark visited, the Mandan and Hidatsa had previously had contact with white Europeans and were helpful to the Corps. The Hidatsa had traveled widely in the Rockies and were able to pass on useful information about the unchartered territory to the West. They drew maps for Lewis and Clark, using whatever materials were available from the floor of a lodge to a tanned skin. Clark copied many of these maps into his journals. They were an indispensable tool for their travels and a beautiful reminder of the perilous and exciting adventure into what were then unknown lands. The villages were abandoned in 1837 after the devastating smallpox outbreaks that decimated the Mandan, Hidatsa and Arikara.

They returned here on Aug 15, 1806 and held a council with the Hidatsa. Colter separated from the group to go upriver with Dickson and Hancock to trap beaver.

Smallpox
Smallpox epidemics almost annihilated prairie Native Americans before Lewis and Clark arrived and continued into the mid-19th century. During the American Revolution from 1775-1782, smallpox spread across America. The Mandan and Hidatsa were hard hit by both smallpox and Indian raids from the Sioux. They fled On-a-Slant village area in 1790 to the mouth of the Knife River. The population of the Mandan and Hidatsa had declined by 75%. Nearby, farther south along the Missouri, the Arikara were also hard hit, killing almost 90% of all the Arikara warriors. The tribes attempted to regroup only to be hit again by smallpox in 1801, but much fewer people were killed perhaps because the groups were starting to develop immunity. When Lewis and Clark arrived, they encountered a much devastated people. For a history of smallpox in the plains, see the report of the North Dakota State Historical Society.

Riverdale

On the S side of the Missouri as it makes its turn towards Montana, the dam sits on ND 200. It's about 26m from Stanton.

> Take a break
>
> I have to mention this place because it covers all the bases, and it's good. There's breakfast, lunch, dinner, ice cream and great coffee. It's not fancy, but its decent. Try **Spillway Coffee House** (504 10th St, 710-654-9540).

- **Garrison Dam and Fish Hatchery**, 530 Hatchery Rd, SD 200, 701-654-7451, 8-3:30, hiking trails, interpretive signs

    Longest dam on the Missouri river and the fifth largest earthen dam in the world. Wetlands Trail Loop and the Lewis and Clark Trail Loop meanders through the cottonwoods, and you can almost imagine Lewis and Clark walking through here and viewing the bald eagles and turkey vultures or the expansive Missouri river views. The corps passed through in two pirogues and six canoes on April 7, 1805, heading west in a large pirogue. Their keelboat, alas, would leave them here and head to St. Louis to send their specimens back to Jefferson. This is a moment to be marked, not only because they are adding to the country's knowledge base in their shipment home but because they are now heading into an area that had little previous white exploration.

Coleharbor

Continuing N from Bismarck, Coleharbor is located on US 83 right before the Missouri River. From Riverdale, you'll travel on ND 200 E about 14 miles. Coleharbor sits just S of Lake Audubon.

- **Audubon National Wildlife Refuge**, 3275 11th St NW, 701-442-5474, https://www.fws.gov/refuge/Audubon/visit/plan_your_visit.html, visitor center (3m N of Coleharbor on Hwy. 83, 8-4:30)

    The almost 15,000 acre refuge includes Lake Sakakawea and lies ten miles east of the Lewis and Clark campsites of April 7-8 1805. In April 1805, the expedition passed the refuge on their way N from Fort Mandan. View wild prairie wildflowers and grasses that may have been growing for Lewis and Clark.

> Take a break
>
> Looking for a steak cooked on a grill? Ribs smoked in the backyard? Burgers and Salads too. Open for lunch and dinner. Try **Coleharbor's Harbor Bar** (Frontage rd, Hwy 83, 701-442-3129).

New Town

You'll move away from the Missouri on US 83N to ND 23 W for 87miles.

✦ **Three Affiliated Tribes Museum**, 336 Main St, 701-627-5154, 10-4pm, mid-April-Nov, closed Sat-Sun. Call ahead. Museum may not be open.

Museum is a heritage center for the Mandan, Hidatsa and Arikara people, all people that Lewis and Clark met with on the expedition. Exhibits include their encounters with Lewis and Clark. Full size reconstructed earth lodge.

Good site for information about The Three Affiliate tribes

🏛 **Crow Flies High Butte Historic Site**, SD 23, 3m W of New Town, 701-627-3550, day use only, interpretive signs.

Once the home of a Hidatsa village, from this butte, French explorers in 1742 viewed the Missouri Valley. The North Dakota badlands are stark and beautiful and worth a view. Clark climbed up here for views of the rest of the corps on April 14, 1805. Lewis wrote,

" I joined the party at their encampment a little after dark . on my arrival Capt Clark informed me that he had seen two white bear pass over the hills shortly after I fired, and that they appeared to run nearly from the place where I shot."

🏛 **Lewis and Clark State Park**, 4904 119th Rd NW, 20m E of Williston S of ND 1804, 701-859-3071, camping, cabins, wifi, picnic shelters, hiking trails, fishing, boating, swimming, playground. Map. If you like wildflowers and want to see some that Lewis identified, this park has a large selection and a plant checklist. This is a really nice park. In the spring it's green and lush with lots of options for shade. And, views of the Dakota badlands to the N. On April 17, 1805, Clark notes that all around this area they have seen signs of the "white bear", what they often called the Grizzly.

Grizzlies on the great plains? It's hard today to imagine the mountain and forest Grizzly bear running around the prairie, but this was once their territory. When Lewis and Clark traveled South and North Dakota, literally millions of bison roamed across the West. And, they died by the hundreds and even thousands when they plunged through thin ice on a river or tumbled over a cliff. The smell of these rotting carcasses was a perfume for the Grizzlies. As the bison were decimated and the plains filled up with gun toting humans the grizzlies headed west and up until North and South Dakota no longer fear their presence.

- **Tobacco Garden Creek Recreation Area**, 4781 ND 1806, 28m N of Watford City, 701-842-4199, restrooms, camping, restaurant, cabins, picnic shelters, wifi, hiking.

   On April 18, 1805, several of the men ran into a bear in this area as they were out hunting.

- **Lewis and Clark Reunion Bay (Reunion Point)**, SD 23 right before you reach the Missouri River, S on 2nd ST NW (toward the town of Sanish) to 92nd St SW, 701-627-4812, interpretive sign

   On their return trip, the corps reunites here on Aug 12 after their July 3, 1806 separation. The day before this reunion, Lewis was shot in the buttocks by one of the corps members, Cruzatte. Cruzatte was blind in one eye and believed he was shooting an elk when he hit Lewis. Lewis had to spend the next couple of weeks lying on his front.

Take a break at the **Better B Café** (204 Main St, 701-627-3888) for diner comfort food like mac and cheese and burgers.

Alexander

Alexander is on US 85, 20m S of Williston. From New Town, cross the Missouri on ND23 W and continue 72 miles.

- **Lewis and Clark Trail Museum**, 102 Indiana Ave E, 701-828-3595, 10-5, 12- Sun, closed Weds. Free.

   Focus is on homesteaders. There are a few Lewis and Clark silhouette statues outside you can pose by.

Take a break
Stop at **James Gang Java**, 102 Indiana Ave, for a snack and cup of coffee.

Williston

Williston sits N of the Missouri River. US 2 comes in from the N and heads W.

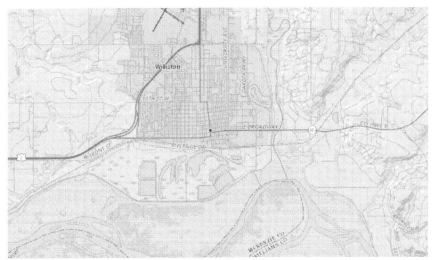

Williston had been growing rapidly in response to oil and gas industry jobs in the surrounding area. With a decline in demand, the city sits in a waiting mode. Meanwhile, however, a lot of development and investment poured into Willison. So, the rather small city includes a Recreation Center, several golf courses, an arts center and sporting complex. It's located on US 85 on the Missouri. Lewis camped several miles SW of Williston on August 8, 1806.

The Missouri Yellowstone Confluence Center, Fort Buford and Fort Union are within 5m of one another. To visit all three, from Williston, head W on US2 and then S on ND 1804. You'll come to the confluence center first on the left (S) then Fort Buford is just around the bend. Back to 1804, continue W to Fort Union.

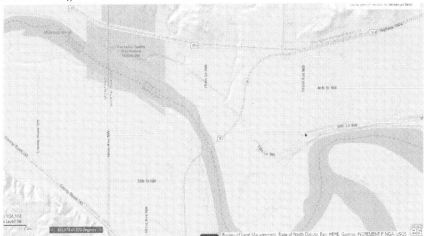

⚑ **Missouri Yellowstone River Confluence Interpretive Center**, 15349 39th Ln NW, 1/2m E of Fort Buford (off county 1804 and 58), 701-572-9034,

9am-6pm summer, 9-4 Weds-Sat rest of the year, $5, $2.50 child. Picnic area, camping, walking trail, bird watching.

Lewis with several of his men moved ahead of the rest of the group on April 25, 1805 to scope out the meeting of the Yellowstone with the Missouri. Exhibits highlight the journey. Enjoy the view that Lewis and Clark would have had of the rivers. Three large murals in the rotunda with quotes from the journals. The East Buford state historic site where Sitting Bull surrendered is next door.

✦ **Fort Union Trading Post NHS**, ND Hwy. 1804, 25m SW of Williston, 701-572-9083, https://www.nps.gov/fous/index.htm, 8am-8pm in summer, and 9-5:30 the rest of the year. The Corps arrived here April 26 1805 to find an abundance of game including buffalo, Elk and Rocky Mountain sheep. The current trading post wasn't built until 1828 where it became the trading headquarters for John Jacob Astor's American fur company.

Bison: When Lewis and Clark traveled through North Dakota, there were at least 30 million bison (American buffalo are actually bison). Lewis and Clark encountered numerous herds, many of them numbering the thousands. Lewis wrote on April 22, 1805,

"I asscended to the top of the cutt bluff this morning, from whence I had a most delightfull view of the country, the whole of which except the vally formed by the Missouri is void of timber or underbrush, exposing to the first glance of the spectator immence herds of Buffaloe, Elk, deer, & Antelopes feeding in one common and boundless pasture. we saw a number of bever feeding on the bark of the trees alonge the verge of the river, several of which we shot, found them large and fat. walking on shore this evening I met with a buffaloe calf which attatched itself to me and continued to follow close at my heels untill I embarked and left it."

Buffalo were the preferred food for the expedition, and one buffalo fed the whole group. But they needed three elk or seven deer. The expedition used the Buffalo for food but also for clothing, blankets, tents, moccasins and pouches or containers. By 1902, there were 700 bison. Today, we have 300,000 after extensive efforts to re-establish the bison. Fish and Wildlife Service provides a timeline of the Bison's decline and recovery.

Montana

Lewis first arrived in what would ultimately become Montana on April 27, 1805. They spent their largest chunk of time in this state; over the span of the trip they were here for about six months. The north-eastern edge where they entered is Missouri River Country, a land of prairies and rivers, little changed since Lewis and Clark passed through. This wide-open landscape with little trace of human habitation is a wonderful place to imagine yourself in Lewis and Clark's boots looking out over the vast landscape wondering what you will encounter next.

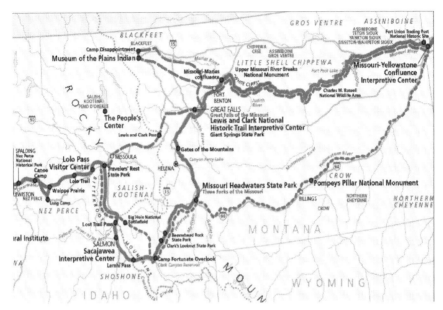

Geology of the area

Montana has great geologic variability. And it would have been strikingly different from the eastern areas familiar to the expedition. Much of the Central and West area the Lewis and Clark traveled through was the result of the massive Glacial Lake Missoula Floods. And, you can't pass through this area without seeing exhibits and interpretive panels that reference this significant geologic event. While Lewis and Clark would have little knowledge of the geologic forces at work when they passed through the area, their speculation was surprisingly on target. Part of their accuracy was a result of oral histories passed on through generations of Native Americans

Lewis and Clark Trail divides: The outbound trail goes North/West the return comes from the South/West from Missoula. For ease of following the guide, I've listed the return S/W route in reverse order from Eastern MT to Western MT.

On the outbound trip, the expedition pretty much travels as one group. But on the return trip, they regularly divide up with Lewis often going one direction and Clark going another. This allows them to cover more territory. Clark and his crew, on the return trip, take the SW route from Traveler's rest (below) while Lewis and his crew take the N route (discussed later).

South/West

On this route, we will be following the Yellowstone South. The Missouri River route is covered later on the N/W route.

Fairview

From Williston, head W on ND1804 and then S on ND58. Fairview is at MT 200 and 58, just S of Fort Union on the North Dakota and Montana border. In fact, the town sits in both ND and MT.

August 3rd, 1806, Clark and his crew spent the night east of Fairview on the Yellowstone River in North Dakota at the mouth of the Charbonneau Creek.

- ✦ **Sundheim Park**, 3m E of Fairview on ND200 along the Yellowstone River, camping, fishing, boating, historic bridge.

    It's worth driving the few miles out here and then heading to the old Fairview bridge for views of the Yellowstone. You can walk out on the bridge or ride your bike.

> Take a break at the **Powder Keg Pizza** place (402 W 9th St, 406-742-5180) and order a Taco Pizza, with light cheese. Almost everything is made in-house. Ice cream also available. Lots of seating and video games. Menu is extensive if pizza doesn't sound good.

Sidney

Sidney, 12m S of Fairview on MT200 and MT16, is the largest town in Eastern Montana and is worth a drive through. It sits in a lush valley just west of the Yellowstone river.

- ✦ **MonDak Heritage Center and Museum**, 120 3rd Ave, 406-433-3500, 10-4, Sat 1-4, closed Sun-Mon, free.

    History, culture, art of the area with many interactive opportunities.

> Take a break at the **Meadowlark Brewing and Public House** (117 S Central Ave, 406-433-2337, http://meadowlarkbrewing.com/), for lunch, dinner or just a beer. Food includes fish tacos and burgers.
>
> **Simply Scrumptious Bakery** (202 E Main, 406-480-05007) for coffee (or cappuccino) and a donut.

- ✦ **Richland Park**, 5m N of Sidney on Hwy. 16, vault toilets, picnic area, playground, nature trail.

- **Elk Island,** 20m S of Sidney on Hwy. 16, turn NE between MP 32 and 33 for one mile on a gravel rd, playground, picnic area, camping, fishing

    On August 2nd, Clark wrote about this part of the Yellowstone River. This is an area where visitors can see the Yellowstone largely as it was when Clark traveled through. Note the sandbars and cottonwoods.

Glendive

From Sidney, continue on MT16 S for 53 miles. Glendive sits right along the Yellowstone. I94 crosses through the town.

⌂ **Interpretive Kiosk**, 808 North Merrill, N of I94 off the eastern exit. Look for the funky mountain men. Kiosk provides detailed information about Clark's trip in 1806.

✦ **Makoshika State Park**, S Merrill Ave/Marsh Rd to E Barry St to S Taylor Ave, S to Snyder St/Makoshika State Park Rd E. 406-377-6256, day use $6, visitor center (10-6), restrooms, camping, picnic areas biking, hiking trails

Badlands formations. Visitor center houses fossil remains of dinosaurs and interpretive displays about the badlands.

Terry

SW of Glendive off I94 at the intersection of old Hwy 10 and ND253, 39 miles.
Clark wrote on July
"the high country is washed into curious mounds and hills and is cut much with reveens..."
Captain Clark Camped 1.5m below the Powder River (S of Terry on W Old Hwy. 10) on the left bank on July 30, 1806. Interpretive sign indicates the spot.

✦ **Prairie County Museum and Evelyn Cameron Gallery**, 101 South Logan, 406-635-4040, Memorial Day-Labor Day, 9-3:30 Mon, Weds, Fri, 1-4 Sat and Sun and by appointment.

Focus is on early pioneer life.

Miles City

SW of Terry on I94, 40 miles. The Yellowstone runs to the W of town. The Yellowstone and Tongue meet in Miles city.

Clark camped near the mouth of the Tongue on July 29, 1806. Follow Water Plant Rd, NW off Main toward the WaterWorks Art Museum (85 Water Plant Rd) to get close to the mouth.

🏛 **Tongue River Interpretive sign**, I94 business route just S of Garryowen Rd at the Fish and Wildlife Parks Dept.

Sign explains Clark's impressions of the Tongue River including his dismay at how horrible the water was to drink here.

✦ **Range Riders Museum**, 435 Main, 406-232-6146, 8am-5pm, April 1-Oct 31,

Both natural and human history of Eastern Montana including dinosaurs, Native Americans and pioneers with a focus on Range Riders. Several replica buildings of a school and a log cabin can be toured. Enormous gun collection.

🏛 **Pirogue Island State Park**, 1m N on MT 59 then 2m E on Kinsey Rd (MT 489), then 2m S on Boone Trail, 406-234-0900, 7am-10pm, vault toilets, interpretive panels, 2.8m of trails, boating, fishing, picnic, hunting. Map.

Clark's group camped here in 1806. Park sits right on the Yellowstone.

Take a break and spend the night in your selection of two charming bed and breakfasts. **Horton House** (1918 Main St, 406-234-4422, http://www.hortonhousebandb.com/index.html) is an upscale bed and breakfast in a stately brick home that is tastefully decorated to reflect historical figures of Eastern Montana. They even have a Lewis and Clark Room! **Yellowstone Bluffs** (27 Buena Vista Dr, 406-234-8012, http://www.yellowstonebluffsbandb.com/) has large spacious rooms and some great outdoor areas in a contemporary setting. A good lunch or dinner (and sports viewing) can be had at **Blackiron Grill** (2901 Boutell St, 406-234-4766, http://www.milescityrestaurant.com/). And get your coffee (and a sandwich) at **Main Street Grind** (713 Main St, 406-234-4664).

Rosebud
Continue on I94 from Miles City for 34 miles.

🏛 **Rosebud Rest Area**, EastboundI94, MM 112, Clark passed through Rosebud on July 28th, 1806 where they were able to kill many buffalo for nourishment. Interpretive sign discusses the importance of the Yellowstone as a travel route from the time of Clark's travel.

Hysham
From Rosebud, N of I94 on Old Hwy 312 for 40 miles.

✦ **Treasure County 89'ers Museum**, 325 Elliott Ave, 406-342-5252, 1-5, closed Sat-Sun

☞ **Yucca Theater**, 324 Elliot Ave, no longer a theater but actually a home, call 406-342-5259 for a tour, or just drive by to see the sculptures.

Local Sculpture Bob Schulze created a series of Lewis and Clark sculptures on the theater lawn including Sacagawea and little pomp (also a sabre tooth tiger and a mammoth—perhaps not quite historically accurate!).

Billings Area

Billings sprawls out from the E of I94, all the way out to Pompey's Pillar to the west on I90. The Interstates intersect on the W side of the city. US 87 comes in from the N. The Yellowstone runs along the S side of the city.

Billings is the largest city in Montana, and it mixes an expected western vibe with a more contemporary get outside and play mentality. It's the center of fishing, skiing, hiking, biking and rock climbing.

See the second page of this brochure for a good Billings overview Map.

☞ **Pompeys Pillar**, 3039 Hwy. 312, 25m E of Billings MT, 406-875-2400, http://www.pompeyspillar.org/, Interpretive Center, 8-5:30 summer, 8-4 Oct., $7 during official hours, restrooms, gift shop, after hours walk-ins are welcome, picnic tables, one mile walk from gate to pillar.

The Corps divided into two groups at Traveler's Rest for the return trip in order to continue with their research and exploration, and Clark and his group of 23 people reached the pillar on July 25, 1806. They named the rock formation after "Pomp" Sacajawea's and Jean Baptiste Charbonneau's child and Clark carved his name, Captain William Clark, with the date, July 25, 1806, on the rock.

Visitors will enjoy the concrete Riverwalk meant to symbolize the Yellowstone river that begins in the parking lot through the interpretive center to the Pillar. Interpretive signs along the Riverwalk quote Clark's journals. Start your visit with the short movie "About the Expedition". Exhibits in the center focus on the Yellowstone river part of the Corp's journey, which includes Sacajawea's contribution. Culture, flora and fauna of the area are also included. Outside, wander alongside the river and observe some of the birds in the riparian areas. The cliffs and pillars are also of geological interest, made of sandstones and shales. The sandstone pillar itself rises 200ft above the river. Continue on the walk to a viewing area over the Yellowstone, the longest free flowing river in the lower 48. Interpretive center is recommended.

* **Pictograph Cave State Park**, 3401 Coburn Rd, exit 452 on I90 at Old US 87, E and then immediately S on Coburn Rd, Billings, 406-254-7342, http://stateparks.mt.gov/pictograph-cave/, 9am-7pm park, 10-6 visitor center. Visitor center, picnic tables, 1/4m loop trail to the caves with interpretive displays.

  2000 year old pictographs on the interpretive trail.

* **Western Heritage Center**, 2822 Montana Ave, Billings, 406-256-6809, http://www.ywhc.org/index.php?p=95, 10-5, closed Sun-Mon, $5 adults, $3 students and seniors, $1 children under 12, cafe.

  The focus is on American Indian and Cowboy history and art. Worth visiting on the third Thursday for the free High Noon lecture series that focuses on a Montana artist, musician or writer.

* **Yellowstone Art Museum**, 401 N 27th St, 406-256-6804, https://www.artmuseum.org/, 10-5 until 8 on Thurs., $15 adult, $6 student.

  The focus is on contemporary art from the northern Rocky Mountain and Plains regions.

* **Museum of Women's History**, 2822 3rd Ave N B-3, 406-248-2015, 1-4 Mon, Tues, Thurs and by appointment, free. Call ahead.

  Exhibits feature women from all walks of life from all areas of the country.

Take a break and eat local and seasonally while downtown at the Fieldhouse (2601 Minnesota Ave, 406-534-2556, https://thefieldhousemt.com/). **The Fieldhouse** serves lunch and dinner and a superb brunch with housemade donuts. Menu changes regularly but the bratwurst is always a great choice. And, I love the meatloaf sandwich. Highly recommended.

Yellowstone County Museum, 1950 Airport Terminal Cir (follow signs for airport entrance and continue around the airport parking areas to the entrance, 406-256-6811, http://www.ycmhistory.org/, 10-5:30, closed Sun-Mon and January.

Exhibits on American Indian and Cowboys as well as the Corps of Discovery. Exhibits focused on Lewis and Clark trace their trail through this area including both inside interpretive exhibits and outside interpretive panels. The museum includes artifacts that were recently located in this area.

On their return trip, Clark was scouring the area for Cottonwood trees he could use to carve out canoes. On July 20, 1806, they finally found some trees in the area and made camp at what is now Park City to build them. The Corps were the victims of horse thief's that evening when possibly some Crow stole half the horses. The area where they build the canoes has been named "Clark's Canoe Camp on the Yellowstone" but it is not open to the public.

The Yellowstone River is the last free flowing river of its size in the lower 48. 670 miles makes its way from Yellowstone National Park in the NW corner of Montana to the Missouri River at the border of North Dakota and Montana. Lewis arrived at the river in April 1805, and we can imagine he thought he'd found that magical body of water that would take him to the Pacific. Game was plentiful and herds of buffalo, elk, deer and antelope roamed freely. The cottonwoods provided needed wood for canoe building. Perhaps it looked a little bit like paradise.

Crow Indian Reservation

S of Billings

✦ **Little Bighorn Battlefield NM**, 756 Battlefield Tour Rd, I 90 E to Hardin, then S on 90 to US 212. https://www.nps.gov/libi/index.htm, 406-638-2621, 8-4pm, 4.5m tour road and walking trail.

While this site has nothing to do with Lewis and Clark, if you are in the area, it's well worth a visit. The battlefield appears as a vast green prairie, but once you visit the visitor center and walk the trail, it feels as if you are present as the 7th Cavalry and the Sioux and Cheyenne make their last stand. Take a tour during the summer. Apsaalooke Tours go into the battlefield, 406-679-0023; ranger tours take place on the patio. I recommend both.

✦ **Big Horn County Historical Museum**, 1163 3rd St. E, Off I90 exit 497, 406-665-1671, https://www.bighorncountymuseum.org/, 8-6 in summer, 9-5 Mon-Fri in winter, $6 adults, $3 students.

24 historic buildings on 35 acres and a variety of exhibits about Little Bighorn, art, pioneer artifacts.

Big Timber

I90 runs to the S of Big Timber. The Yellowstone River is to the N. I like Big Timber as a base camp. It's got a nice downtown, a small western town feel and the scenery surrounding the town mixes river and mountains.

Clark wrote about seeing the intersection of the Boulder River and the Big Timber Creek and where they empty into the Yellowstone on the NE side of town. You can't really see this intersection anymore, but at the Otter Creek Fishing Access Site on the Yellowstone, you are close to where the Boulder River enters the Yellowstone.

🏛 **Crazy Mountain Museum**, 2 South Frontage Rd, off I90, 406-932-5126, http://crazymountainmuseum.com/index.shtml, open Memorial Day-End of Sept. 10-4:30. Call ahead, hours are subject to change.

Limited Corps of Discovery exhibits (organized in the Norwegian Stabbur building) including a painting by Jack Hines of Clark and Sacajawea and a Lewis and Clark garden that is worth visiting. It includes the plants from Montana that Clark mentions in his journals. Outside, an interpretive panel of Clark the cartographer and the expedition are on display.

Take a Break at the **Grand Hotel Saloon** (139 McLeod St, 406-932-4459) for a western themed steak dinner or at the **Big Timber Bakery** (121 McLeod St, 406-932-3524) for breakfast, wood-fired pizza or a brownie. The bakery is also a great place to pick up sandwiches to go. The Grand Hotel is not a bad place to spend the night. It's a restored 1890 hotel and has a lot of charm. And, stop into **Cole Drug** (136 McLeod St, 406-932-5316), an old fashioned soda fountain, for a berry shake or a soda.

Livingston Area

Livingston is immediately off I90, 35m W of Big Timber; access downtown on US89. The Yellowstone River runs to the S of town.

Clark camped on the Yellowstone River near Livingston in July 1806 as he headed home with Sacagawea and others from the party. Today, Livingston is the center of outdoor activities. Hiking, rafting, fishing can all be found nearby.

- **Sacajawea Park Livingston**, 229 River Dr, Livingston, from US89, head E toward the river and you'll hit River Dr. At the intersection of River Dr and Yellowstone St, picnic tables, tennis courts, restrooms, fishing, skateboard park, playground.

  On July 15, 1806, Clark and his party, including Sacajawea, came through the area on their way to Clark's Canoe Camp on the Yellowstone (see above). A 9ft bronze statue by Mary Michael of Sacagawea and Pomp on a horse commemorates their visit and an interpretive panel provides a brief overview of Sacagawea's role. It's a beautiful park, and a great place to stop for a picnic.

- **Yellowstone Gateway Museum**, 118 W Chinook St, 406-222-4184, https://yellowstonegatewaymuseum.org/, 10-5 summer, 10-5 Thurs-Sun the rest of the year.

  Exhibits on the native Americans of the area and local history but one room is dedicated to the Corps of Discovery and follows their journey along the Yellowstone in Park County in July 1806. Exhibits include plant and animal life on the exploration. Includes a replica canoe.

> Take a break in Livingston at **Gil's Goods** (207 W Park St, 406-222-9463, http://gilsgoods.com/) with a fresh, local meal any time of the day including wood fired pizza (the Buffalo Gil is good and spicy). Good pastries as well and worth a stop for a couple of to-go road trip bites. For a taste of the old west, **The Stockman** (118 N Main, 406-222-8455) is always a good choice for a burger in a cowboy atmosphere. Beer at **Neptune's Brewery** (119 N L St, 406-222-7837), including a great Chocolate Porter, compliments the pub menu. Looking for fast food? **Marks In and Out** (801 W Park St, 406-222-7744) has burgers, fries and shakes and great out door seating or take a bag to go.

☐ **Shields River and Valley,** US 89 N of US191 to MM4.

The Shields river is a tributary of the Yellowstone. Head out on US 89 and cross the one-lane historic steel bridge over the river. Clark named this river and valley after John Shields from the expedition. Clark and his crew, including Shields, came through this area in July 1806. Shields was from Kentucky, one of the only married men from the expedition and was an excellent blacksmith and gunsmith.

☐ **Bozeman Pass**, 12m W of Livingston on I90. 5702ft elevation. Interpretive panel on Sacajawea.

The Corps crossed the pass on July 15, 1806 guided by Sacagawea on an old buffalo road. The group built their canoes for their downriver trip.

Bozeman

I90 W from Livingston 26 miles.

> Take a break at one of the many local dining options on 191 downtown (Main St). There are so many good options, it's very difficult to single anything out. And, new ones just keep coming. Your best bet is to check out the most recent Trip Advisor Reviews. **Cateye** (23 N Trace Ave, 406-587-8844) is a lively, colorful breakfast and lunch option. Try something with the chili verde. **Western Café** (443 E Main St, 406-587-0436) has been largely untouched by Bozeman's modernization and is a trip back in time and cowboy nostalgia.

✦ **Gallatin History Museum**, 317 West Main St, 406-522-8122, http://www.gallatinhistorymuseum.org/, 11-5, Tues-Sat, $7.50 adult, $5 child.

Research library includes a special Lewis and Clark collection. Housed in an old jail, museum's focus is town history including a reconstructed log cabin, Indian artifacts and a model of an old fort.

- ★ **Museum of the Rockies**, 600 W Kaby Blvd, 406-994-2251, https://www.museumoftherockies.org/, 8am-6pm summer, closes at 5pm rest of the year, $14.50 adult, $9.50 children,

  Heirloom garden with flowers from the Corps of discovery in the Tinsley House. Main focus is dinosaur fossils, but local history is also included as well as a Living History farm. Keelboat replica like Lewis and Clark used.

North Route from Fort Union

This is the main route that the expedition took on their way West and Lewis' route (mostly) on the way back.

Montana

Entering Montana on US2, the Missouri is to the S where the corps traveled. By Culbertson, the river is running much closer to the highway. As you follow Hwy 2, you'll be paralleling the river. After Culbertson, you'll enter the Missouri Breaks, some of the most ruggedly beautiful riverside terrain you'll see.

In far Eastern Montana, many of the original campsites have been destroyed by significant changes in the Missouri River's flow over the last 200 years. Many of the sites listed below are near or overlook where a campsite was believed to exist, but most are difficult to access and provide almost no interpretation. If you are going to explore this area, I highly recommend the *Benchmark Montana Atlas* for detailed maps. And, load up with gas, water and food because services can be few and far between.

On this stretch of the corps' expedition, they had no contact with Indians though they did observe signs. However, there was a noticeable increase in mishaps with nature, specifically with grizzly bears and weather. While you are unlikely to encounter the first, be prepared for the later. Montana can still dish out consider weather diversity and extremes.

As you get closer to Fort Peck, the access and interpretation increases. This area of Eastern Montana has also been affected by the oil boom in the Fort Union Geological formation (see below).

Nohly

- **Nohly and Snowden Bridge**, SD 58 S from Buford into Montana to CR 147 NW. The actual site is near the bridge over the Missouri, one mile S of Nohly.

  On April 27th, 1805 the expedition entered Montana in six canoes and two pirogues. They camped one mile below the bridge on the opposite bank for the first night in Montana. Lewis noted his appreciation of the rock formations.

Bainville

On US 2, 30m W of Williston

- **Otis Creek**, 9m SW Bainville off CR 147, not accessible.

April 28th, the corps camped across from Otis Creek after making good time with fair winds. They traveled over 24miles on the 28th. They saw great quantities of Beaver. Clark walked along the bluffs that run along the Missouri here noting their appearance and color in his journal. Grizzly bears were also sited. This area of the trail is very much the same as it was when Lewis and Clark passed through. Note the rock formations and the coal seams that streak the buttes and hills. Lewis notes these in his journal.

Fort Union Geological Formation

The dominant geological formation encountered in Eastern MT and Western ND is the coal bearing Fort Union Formation (hence, nearby Williston South Dakota's value for the oil industry). The formation actually covers about as much territory as the state of Texas. Rivers flowing east deposited sediments about 65 million years ago creating a shallow but huge bowl filled with wet, humid, tropical jungles. Frequent rains washed sediments into the bowl and continued to do so for 10 million years creating layers and layers of sediment that mixed with the skeletons of sea creatures and the loam of vegetation. Over time, the sediment turned into the coalbeds. Some of the built up layers are exposed in the area, forming cross sections of massive rocks up and down the Missouri and Yellowstone.

Culbertson

US 2 and MT 16, 43m W of Williston ND

- ⚑ **Culbertson Bridge Access**, 3m S of Culbertson on MT16, day use, picnic area, toilet, interpretive sign.

Take a break at the **Wild West Diner** (20 6th St E, 406-787-5374) for breakfast or lunch and most likely you'll be eating with locals. Check out what they are ordering and copy them! Sandwiches are simple and served with homemade chips

---

- 🏚 **Big Muddy Creek**, W of Culbertson, Hwy 2 over the bridge on Muddy Creek and turn N on Indian Rd to the banks of the creek.

April 29th, Lewis opted to walk along the shore and killed his first grizzly. He continued to see lots of wildlife from pronghorns to elk. They camped just above the creek. Big Muddy is one of three Creeks, along with the Milk River and the Poplar River, that flow from Canada to the Gulf of Mexico.

Lewis wrote, *"I walked on shore with one man. About 8 A.M. we fell in with two brown or yellow [white] bear, both of which we wounded. one of them made his escape; the other, after my firing on him, pursued me 70 or 80 yards but fortunately had been so badly wounded that he was unable to pursue so closely as to prevent my charging my gun; we again repeated our fir[e] and killed him."*

Brockton

20 miles W of Culbertson on Hwy. 2

- 🏛 **Brockton**, on the Western edge of town, turn south on South Track Rd to the banks of the Missouri

  While most of the expedition continued to sail through the Missouri, Clark, Charbonneau and Sacagawea walked on the shore, camping near Brockton the night of April 30th 1805, Lewis shot a big Bull elk.

- 🏛 **Elkhorn Point**, W from Brockton about 6m on Hwy 2 to MT 480 S and before the bridge, turn west on the dirt road toward the riverbank to the end of the road,

  The corps spent the night of May 1, 1805.

- 🏛 **Hwys 2 and 251**, 8m W of Brockton, After a snowing morning, the group got a late start, made five miles and camped on the N bank on May 2, 1805.

Poplar

US 2, 14 miles W of Brockton

- 🏛 **Poplar,** Hwy 2 W to Poplar passing through town to the western edge of the city and turn left on CR 34 to the end and then SE on CR 17-1054 heading S to the Missouri River.

  They camped at the intersection of the Poplar and Missouri on May 3, 1805.

- 🏛 **Wolf Point**, Hwy. 2 W about 10m from Poplar to MT 13 turn S to the Missouri River, 6m SE of Wolf Point, day use, picnic area, toilet, fishing, hiking, interpretive panel.

  On May 5, 1805, the expedition camped just S of this town. They saw a great deal of game.

Take a break in Wolf Point at the **Wolf Point Café** (217 Main St, 406-653-1388) for good, local lunch and dinner. They serve homemade pizza, burgers and daily specials.

Oswego

US 2, 33 miles W of Poplar.

- 🏛 **Oswego**, SW of the town, exact site not known.

  After making good time, they camped on May 6th near here noting how beautiful the plains were.

🏛 **Frazer**, 5m SW of Frazer off the S end of Fourstar Rd. They camped here on May 7th.

Glasgow

On Hwy. 2, just past the turn off to the Fort Peck area. Largest town in the area.

🏛 **Valley County Pioneer Museum**, 816 US2, 406-228-8692, http://www.valleycountymuseum.com/, Summer 9-5pm, closed Sun; fall 1-5 Tues-Fri., $3 adult, $2 students.

Local history including railroad, Native American and agriculture displays as well as a Lewis and Clark exhibit.

> Take a break at **Eugene's Pizza** (193 Klein Ave, 406-228-8552), making pizzas for the last 50 years. Good pizzas, wings, chicken dinners, for lunch and dinner. They make a good Taco pizza. And, people swear by the sauerkraut pizza, The Henry J. . . Spend the night at the historic **Rundle Suites** (208 5th St, 406-228-2800, https://www.rundlesuites.com/) decorated in standard motel décor but with upscale accents. They rent bikes and have an exercise room.

Fort Peck

Once a real fort in the 1860's, today Fort Peck refers to the area at the head of the 1500 miles of shoreline around Fort Peck Lake and Dam. Map.

🏛 **Milk River Confluence**, at the intersection of MT 117 and US 2 you can see the Milk, the confluence is just a few miles S. You can get closer on the unmarked roads to the east of MT 117 (see below).

The Corps arrived at this confluence, called by the Hidatsas, "AH-mah-tah-ru-shush-sher" or "the river which scolds at all others" on May 8, 1805. May 9-13 the corps stayed in places now under water. On the 9th, Lewis wrote about a particularly dry arm of Fort Peck, "the most extraordinary site I ever beheld. It is as wide as the Missouri is at this place. . . and not containing a single drop of running water".

The white color of this river is how it got its name, and Lewis notes this color in his journals. The Milk River begins near Glacier National Park and travels 732 miles to the confluence with the Missouri. This is one of the few missed opportunities for the corps. Lewis, on his return journey, decides to follow the Marias believing it to be the northern most tributary of the Missouri. It wasn't. The Milk actually goes much further north and had the corps followed it, the US might now include some of S. Canada.

🏛 **Milk River Observation Point**, from the intersection of US 2 and state highway 117, follow 117 for 10.7m to the intersection with Yellowstone Rd. Go south and east on Yellowstone Road for about 2.7 miles to the intersection with MT State Highway 24. Turn left and go easterly on MT State Highway 24 for about 3.0 miles to the intersection with Tower Hill Road. Turn left and go northeast on Tower Hill Road for about 1.75 miles to a Y-junction. Bear left and go northeast and uphill for about 0.25 miles to the parking area on the right for the Milk River Observation Point. Road can be difficult. If you don't have four-wheel drive, tread carefully. From the parking area, head northerly up a steep trail for about 200 yards to the top of the ridge and four interpretive signs.

The point stands at one of the highest points in northeastern MT with great views of the Milk River/Missouri Confluence. A hiking trail leads to the point, which includes a Lewis and Clark interpretive sign.

As they continued up the Missouri over the next several days, they would encounter real mishap on May 14th when one of their pirogues, steered by the inexperienced Charbonneau, turned over spilling out not only contents and passengers but also journals. Sacagawea was one of the passengers who spilled into the river, clutching not only her baby son but also the journals. Pierre Cruzatte was able to right the boat and save Sacagawea, Pomp and the journals.

✦ **Fort Peck Interpretive Center**, 157 Yellowstone Rd, 406-526-3493, https://www.visitmt.com/listings/general/dinosaur-museum/fort-peck-interpretive-center-and-museum.html, 9am-5pm summer, 10-4 winter Tues-Fri,

The two largest aquariums in Montana as well as exhibits on dinosaurs, flora and fauna and the construction of the Fort Peck Dam. The interpretive center is one of the best I've seen at a dam. The group camped near the dam on May 8th.

Lewis and Clark Overlook, 1/2m E of the dam powerhouse on Hwy. 24, picnic area, restrooms. Interpretive signs.

Duck Creek, 2m SW of Fort Peck on Hwy 24, picnic tables, toilet. Camped near here on May 9th

Snow Creek, accessible only on the water.

They camped above snow creek on May 14-16. The closest access to this point is at the Charles M Russell National Wildlife Refuge, which is to the N of this point. They had a serious interaction with a Bear and almost lost one of their pirogues on the 14th, so the 15th became a day of rest and drying out all the wet materials from the pirogue.

Charles M Russell National Wildlife Refuge, the refuge is huge, covering 1.1 million acres. Headquarters are located in Lewistown. Fort Peck Wildlife Station, Hwy 24 in Fort Peck, 7am-4pm, hunting, fishing, auto tour, trails, Map.

The corps camped at 20 sites within the refuge from May 9-24th. Sadly, most of the sites now lie under the Missouri.

> For in-depth discovery of this area, you really need to get on the water. One guided choice is offered by Wilderness Inquiry (612-676-9400, https://www.wildernessinquiry.org/itinerary/montanas-missouri-river-family-canoe/) who will provide a guided 6-day canoe trip through the area.

Lewis and Clark Camp at Slaughter River, Big Sandy, off Judith Landing Rd Hwy. 236

Lewis and Clark stopped here on the way to and from the Pacific on May 29, 1805 and July 29 1806. They found over 100 bison carcasses at the river and believing they've been slaughtered, the river got its name. But, the bison had actually drowned when an ice dam broke. Today, the river is called "Arrow Creek" and is located in the Upper Missouri River Breaks. Accessible by boat and by a rough overland route with permission from the BLM.

Missouri Breaks Area

406-622-4000,   https://www.blm.gov/visit/upper-missouri-river-breaks-national-monument

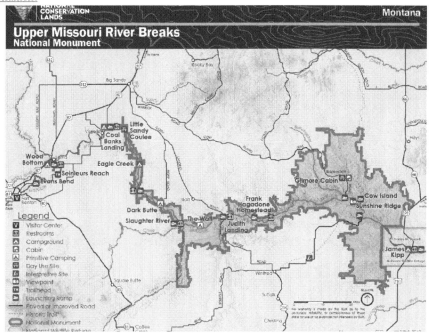

(Map is from the US Department of the Interior, https://www.blm.gov/documents/montana-dakotas/public-room/map/upper-missouri-river-breaks-national-monument)

Continuing from the Western Edge of the Charles M Russell National Wildlife Refuge, the breaks stretch to the W across largely undeveloped land and water to US 87 to the W and MT 60 to the S. The breaks are marginally accessible on US 191 on the E side. And from the W side, US 87 to MT 236 which turns into a gravel road to Judith Landing. The best trips in the area are by water. Visitors can plan their own trip or take a guided trip. (See Upper Missouri Breaks listing under Fort Benton for specific information on the W side of the Breaks).

Great Falls Rafting provides half and full day trips to the breaks that includes Lewis and Clark sites.

Big Wild Adventures, 406-848-7000, provides week long canoe adventures of the breaks.

Upper Missouri River 406-261-3297, offers both day and multi-day trips. This service has the most diverse options.

Unlike Eastern Montana with its meadows and wide-open spaces, the breaks is a mixture of rugged topography, spectacular scenery and water. Lewis and Clark entered the breaks on May 9, 1805 at present day Fort Peck. The Upper Missouri Breaks National Monument covers 375,000 acres in Central Montana. Missouri Breaks refers to a break in the land made by Coulees as water from the river spills out and creates "fingers" across the land.

The corps stayed in the breaks area from the last week of May through the first two weeks of June. They stayed in the lower breaks on May 25 on Power Plant Rd, and on May 26th on Windsor Creek. On the 27th, they stayed at Safford Ferry Rd. And, on the 28th on the Judith River.

●   **White Cliffs of the Missouri**

On May 27th, the Corps entered the Upper Missouri Breaks. They noted the amazing geological formations they passed. These rocks are truly startling to the first-time visitor, their white pinnacles, buttes and rock formations tower over the Missouri river mixed in with some darker rocks and towering walls, many made by magna pushed through the softer sedimentary rock. The sandstone was deposited as sand during the Cretaceous Period. The dark rock is shale. The white sandstone is Virgelle Member, and its topped by hard sandstone, protecting the white rock from erosion. Some have called this area, "The most beautiful place on earth" (Stephen Ambrose). Rafting, canoeing or boating is the primary way to see the cliffs (see listings above for options).

Fort Benton Area

Visitor Information, http://www.fortbenton.com/

This is the head of the navigation of the Missouri River. Today, Fort Benton is a town in the midst of either revival or decline—depending on how you look at it. The actual fort at Fort Benton has been restored, and the downtown offers a few restaurants, a walking trail along the river with multiple interpretive panels and a bridge that has been converted to a walking path. Fort Benton is a charming town and can work as a base camp for the surrounding area.

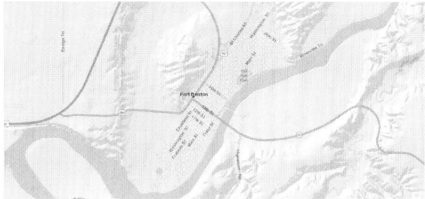

Take a break in historic lodging in Fort Benton at the **Grand Union Hotel** (1 Grand Union Square, 406-622-1882, http://grandunionhotel.com/) or the Pioneer Lodge. These are distinctly different options but both are centrally located and provide solid basecamps. The

Grand Union is all the name implies, leather, wood, brick and antique luxury remind visitors of a much earlier era. **The Pioneer Lodge** is an old mercantile, built in 1916. When you walk in, you may feel like you are entering an old mercantile and rooms are standard motel style with modern amenities including air conditioning and cable. They do have a Lewis and Clark Suite, though the rooms are not particularly distinctive in their décor.

The Corps was in this area on June 11-13th, 1805. Because of the falls, the corps could go no further on the river. The corps walked along the river here (not on the nice path you'll be enjoying!) and, across from the old fort, Lewis, Drouillard and the Field Brothers met Sargent Ordway's party on July 19th 1806.

🏛 **State of Montana's Lewis and Clark Memorial**, on the levee, the large statue by Bob Scriver looks out over the Missouri.

✦ **Missouri Breaks Interpretive Center**, 701 7th St, 406-622-4000, https://www.blm.gov/learn/interpretive-centers/missouri-breaks-interpretive-center, 8am-4:30, closed from Nov-April, $5, children free. Hands on exhibits, a 20-minute film, 3-D scale models of the Breaks and a river trail. Boating information.

Small visitor center with basic visiting information for the area, particularly for those hoping to canoe. If you are headed out on the water, be sure to ask about the "EarthCache trail", 19 interpretive sites throughout the breaks for those floating the area. Check out the flora and fauna collection that depicts specimens Lewis and Clark collected on their trip. 20-minute film on the white cliffs highlights the beauty of the area that most people won't see without getting out into the breaks. Be sure to check out the sidewalks around the center which include animal tracks and a map.

✦ **Fort Benton Museums**, 1205 20th St S, 406-622-5316, 406-622-4000, http://www.fortbentonmuseums.com/, generally open from the end of May to the end of Sept 8am-noon, closed weekends. Winter hours by appointment, fees. Several museums including Historic Old Fort Benton, the Museum of the Northern Great Plains, and the Museum of the Upper Missouri are contained in the Fort Benton Museums group. Settler and Native American history dominates. The Fort is located in the city park and includes restrooms (even when the fort itself isn't open), picnic tables and the river walk. You can also walk to downtown from the park area and get lunch or an ice cream cone.

The Museum of the Upper Missouri, http://www.fortbentonmuseums.com/mum.html, Steamboat history on the Missouri.

The Museum of the Northern Great Plains, http://www.fortbentonmuseums.com/ag.html, Focus is on three families homesteading the area. Small exhibit on Decision Point. This is a museum that kids often like because there are many life size dioramas.

Loma

8m N of Fort Benton on US 87

⚐ **Decision Point**, S of Loma on US87 to Loma Ferry Rd S, 406-622-4000, a dirt road leads to the parking area, but gravel keeps it passable even in wet weather. Read the interpretive panels in the parking area then climb the 1/4m trail to the overlook of the confluence of the Marias and Missouri river. A short side trail leads to an overlook to the West.

The corps camped below the overlook from June 3-12, 1805 and climbed up on the bluff to make the decision of which river was the Missouri. The North branch was muddy and looked like the Missouri they had come from while the South ran clear. Lewis and Clark tended to believe the clear water was the Missouri. They spent five days exploring the branches and determined that the south branch was the Missouri. Luckily, they were correct. The corps stashed supplies for later use. Visitors can still see the confluence and attempt to make their own decision.

Take a break

Lunch at **Ma's Café** (203 US 87, 406-739-4400) in Loma is a good bet. The food is good, reliable comfort food but be sure to end your meal with a slice of homemade pie. We always take a piece of pie with us on the road.

🏛 **Upper Missouri Breaks National Monument,** https://www.blm.gov/programs/national-conservation-lands/montana-dakotas/upper-missouri-river-breaks, Map

Spanning 149m of the Upper Missouri River, 350,000 acres of Central Montana, 149 miles of the Upper Missouri River, six wilderness study areas, both the Lewis and Clark and Nez Perce Trails, it's amazing just how many people have never heard of this spectacular national monument. But, this anonymity has maintained the area largely like it was when Lewis and Clark first ventured into the park. Much of the park is only accessible through gravel or unimproved roads or along the river, but the less adventurous will also find access at various points.

Start at the **Missouri Breaks Interpretive Center** in Fort Benton (701 7th St, 406-622-4000), Lewiston (920 Northeast Main, 406-538-1900) or Havre Field Offices (3990 Hwy 2 West, 406-262-2820), get maps, ask questions and plan a trip that meets your needs. There are multiple boat access points, several companies offer guided options and those who don't want to use the water can visit **The Charles M. Russell National Wildlife Refuge** (see separate listing).

Captain Clark wrote about the badlands saying, *"This country may with propriety, I think, be termed the Deserts of America, as I do not conceive any part can ever be settled, as it is deficient in water, timber, and too steep to be tilled."*

- **Coal Banks Landing**, Off US 87 to Virgelle Ferry Rd N, 406-622-4000, $10, camping, picnic tables, vault toilets

    Interpretive Center and interpretive markers about Lewis and Clark's passage through the area in spring 1805.

Browning Area

Browning is at the intersection of US 2 and US89. From Fort Benton it is directly W about 140 miles.

Browning Chamber of Commerce, 406-338-4015, www.browningchamber.com

- **Camp Disappointment**, US 2, MM 233, located on the Blackfeet Reservation, 406-338-7737,

    Lewis, Drouillard and Joseph and Reubin Field stayed at the northernmost point of the trip, Camp Disappointment, from July 22-26 1806. The disappointment refers to Lewis' failed hope that he would locate a tributary of the Missouri River that extended to 50 north latitude thus allowing the US to extend its northern boundaries. Interpretive board is 4m S of the actual campsite and explains the meaning of Camp Disappointment.

- **Museum of the Plains Indian**, US 2 and 89 West, 19 Museum Loop, Browning, 406-338-2230, https://www.doi.gov/iacb, 9am-4:45 summer, closed Sun-Mon; 10-4:30 closed Sat-Sun, $5 in summer, free the rest of the year.

    Historic arts from tribal people of the Northern Plains.

- **Lodgepole Gallery and Tipi Village**, 245 US Hwy 89, 2.5m W of Browning on Hwy 89, 406-338-2787, http://www.blackfeetculturecamp.com/, contemporary and traditional art. Blackfeet history tour is also offered.

Take a break at the **Lodgepole Tipi Village** (406-338-3787, http://www.blackfeetculturecamp.com/) and experience an alternative lodging experience, sleeping in a tipi, and, if you talk with the proprietors or take a tour, an alternative perspective on the Natives relationship with the Anglo-Americans.

Dupuyer/Valier

43m SE of Browning, US89 S to MT44 E.

♥ **Two Medicine Fight Site**, 16 Old Person Rd, 18m N of Valier, The site is not open to the public but a historic marker is available at US 89 just N of MT 44..

> **The Blackfeet**
> After leaving Camp Disappointment on July 26, 1806, Lewis, Drouillard and Joseph and Reubin Field ran into eight members of the Blackfeet tribe. They decided to camp together. While they were camping, Lewis explained that America would soon be providing guns to the Nez Perce and Shoshone, without realizing that these were the enemies of the Blackfeet. In the morning, the men woke to find the Blackfeet stealing their weapons, they gave chase, and in the process Reubin Field killed one of the Indians and in the ensuing struggle Lewis killed another Native American. The Blackfeet fled. The Blackfeet returned to their tribe and explained the American plans to arm other tribes. The Blackfeet now viewed the Americans as enemies.

Chester

US 2, 76 m E of Valier.

July 1806, Lewis and his party were the first recorded white men to enter this area.

♥ **Lewis and Clark Gazebo/Overlook**, Four Interpretive Signs, 18m S on MT 366, near Stanford Park on the Marias River

The signs detail Lewis' trip through the area on the Marias in both 1805 and 1806. Gorgeous sweeping views over the area that appears largely as it did when Lewis was here on July 20th, 1806.

✦ **Liberty County Museum**, 230 Second St. E, 406-759-5256, 1-5, 7-9 daily, mid-May to Labor Day, free. A combination of pioneer and Native American history.

▩ **Tiber Reservoir**, 12m S of Chester on MT223 then 7m W on County Rd.

Lewis camped here on July 19th, 1806 on his trip to Camp Disappointment

Shelby

Intersection of I15 and US 2

Lewis camped 5m SW of Shelby on the Marias River on July 20th, 1806

Shelby Visitor Information Center, 100 Montana Ave, 406-434-7184

▩ **Marias Museum of History**, 1129 1st N, 406-424-2551, 1-7 Mon-Fri, 1-4 Sat. Call for off-season hours.

Focus is on homesteading and local history. Includes exhibit on Lewis and his small party as they passed through this area in July, 1806.

> Take a break in Shelby at the **Frontier Bar and Supper Club** (29804 US 2, 406-432-3600). Don't be put off by the outside's limited appeal, but head inside for good comfort food like Prime Rib, steak. Stick with tried and true local options. For fast food, go to the **Dash Inn** (702 W. Roosevelt Hwy, 406-434-5888) and get a hot dog and shake and enjoy it on the outside picnic table or in the car.

Cut Bank

The North Fork of the Marias is now known as Cut Bank Creek. It is this fork that Lewis led his small group of explorers up to find its beginning.

Lewis camped at this north branch on July 21, 1806. Cut Bank features a large mural about the expedition.

🏛 **Glacier County Historical Museum & Archive**, 107 Old Kevin Hwy, 406-873-4904,

Includes Lewis and Clark exhibits but focus is on homesteading and oil prospecting in the area.

Great Falls Area

Great Falls in central Montana is a great place to get started on the Lewis and Clark trail and to use as a base camp. The small airport is served by most major airlines, and is quite easy to get to and from. I15 runs along the west side of the city and Hwy. 87 serves the east, north and south. The Missouri runs through the center of the city. The sprawling town of housing developments, strip malls and oil related businesses is thriving and offers a full range of services, including a wide-ranging trail system and multiple Lewis and Clark sites. Great Falls is known as the "electricity city", and if you visit the falls, you'll see ample evidence of all the hydroelectricity the town generates.

One of the few disappointments in Great Falls is that the falls have been so dramatically changed from when Lewis and Clark came through. During their journey, there were five powerful falls, four have been damned and in that process, one has been submerged. As you view the dams, it's difficult to imagine past the hydroelectric development what the falls might have looked like to the expedition. And, what an obstacle they must have posed! In order to portage around the 18 miles that the falls covered, the corps made wheels out of trunks of cottonwoods and rolled their canoes and goods (an excellent place to see these contraptions is at the **Lewis and Clark Interpretive Center** in Great Falls). The ground was a mess of prickly pear cactus and rocks and mud, a continual assault on their feet. And they also experienced significant hail while portaging the area. Somehow, the group managed to trek the goods around the falls without losing anybody even if they were all a little worse for wear. There much shorter return trip would be a significantly easier, 8-day journey from Traveler's rest to the Falls.

Visitor Center, 100 1st Ave N, Lower Level Suite, 406-761-4436 (15 Overlook Dr, 406-771-0885), 8-5pm, closed Sat-Sun. Access the river's edge trail here.

- ✦ **River's Edge Trail**, 1700 River Drive N for fold-up map, http://thetrail.org/, almost 60 miles of trail along the Missouri River for biking, walking, rollerblading. Accesses many of the sites in the Great Falls area. Pick up a brochure at the visitor center. See sites below for reference. Brochure. Map.

- ⌖ **Broadwater Overlook**, off 10th Ave at the river, take overlook drive, look for the big flag.

  Note the Lewis, Clark, York and Seaman bronze sculpture, "Explorers at the Portage", done by Bob Scriver. 35 stone plaques commemorate the members of the expedition. The mountains in the distance are the Lewis Range of the Rockies.

- ⌖ **West Bank Park**, off 4th St NE across the railroad tracks and right on gravel road .4m. Interpretive signs.

  Lewis encountered a Grizzly bear who chased him into the Missouri River on June 14, 1805. Lewis aggressively attacked the bear, who turned and ran.

- ⌖ **Black Eagle Falls and Dam**, off River Drive N and accessible on the River's Edge Trail

  One of the falls around which Lewis and Clark had to portage. Here, on June 13th 1805, Lewis encountered a grizzly who surprised him while he was killing a buffalo. Lewis fended off the grizzly with a spear.

The Dam construction began in 1890. Through the early 1900's the Anaconda Copper company built a massive smelter here. It was removed in the 1980's.

 ♦ **Lewis and Clark National Historical Park Interpretive Center**, 4201 Giant Springs Rd, Great Falls, 406-727-8733, https://www.fs.usda.gov/recarea/hlcnf/recarea/?recid=61458, 9-5 Oct-May, closed Mon. May-Sept 9-6pm. $8, under 15 free, picnic tables. No food or drink. Access to river trail.

Watch one of the introductory videos (or both, if you have the time) and join a ranger for a program. Explore the hands-on exhibits including a two-story diorama of the Great Falls portage. There are a lot of other options in the 25,000 square foot interpretive center, so try to plan several hours to visit. An excellent exhibit shows how the boats, almost life sized, are portaged. And another allows visitors to attempt to pull the boats themselves. Several trails are also available. A nature trail winds around the top of the bluff outside the center. Another trail, the South Bluff Trail, leads to a river overlook. The 2.1m Giant Springs Loop takes in the interpretive center and the nearby Giant Springs. This is a must see destination for Lewis and Clark fans.

Objects of the Journey

In Jefferson's instructions, he requested that Lewis would bring back objects that would enrich scientific knowledge. He would also bring many objects with him necessary to gather cultural, historical and natural knowledge. Jefferson called these objects, "Objects of the Journey." Visitors to the Lewis and Clark trail will see some of these objects or imitations of them, at least, along the route. But, what happened to the originals?

Lewis and Clark managed not only to collect a variety of animals and plants but also transported them to the East. Charles Wilson Peel restored many of the animals, and they were displayed in his museum. When the museum failed, the collection was sadly divided among the Boston Museum and the PT Barnum Museum. After the failure of the Boston Museum and the fire at PT Barnum, what was left ended up at the Peabody Museum at Harvard. As a result, we have lost many of the collected specimens.

 ♦ **Lewis and Clark Trail Heritage Foundation Office and Historical Library**, 4201 Giant Springs Rd, 406-454-1234, http://www.lewisandclark.org/index.php, 9am-5pm M-F, dedicated to Lewis and Clark topics. Call for an appointment. This is less a place to visit then a place to get information or do research. It is probably the foremost center on Lewis and Clark topics.

🏛 **Giant Springs State Park**, 4803 Giant Springs Rd, located just downstream from the Interpretive Center, 406-727-1212, 8am-sunset. Restrooms, picnic tables, playground. Map Accessible on the River's Edge Trail.

Visitors can park at Giant Springs, visit the hatchery, walk past the springs and then take a 1/4m trail up the river to the Interpretive Center. Largest fresh water springs in the world with 156 gallons of water every 24 hours.

Lewis discovered the Springs on June 18, 1805 as he attempted to determine the length of the portage.

🏛 **Rainbow Falls**, can be viewed from both sides of the river on Giant Springs Rd (from River Rd) on the S side or on Rainbow Dam Rd (from Wire Mill Rd) on the N side, both accessible from 15th St NE. The dam itself is accessible on the N side, or follow the River's Edge Trail to the top of the Gorge, around 1.4m, on the South shore of the Missouri River, drive past Giant Springs to the rainbow falls overlook.

The dam here was built to power the mines in Butte. Downstream 1/4 mile is Crooked falls. There are two overlooks here which give excellent views of the falls. When the water is running high, the falls literally thunder over the dam. Colter falls, the fifth falls that the expedition located, is buried in the water of Rainbow Dam but can be seen when the water is really low. The dam was installed in 1920 and reduced the height and power of the falls that Lewis and Clark once viewed. But the 45ft waterfalls are still beautiful. The falls are visible as you hike along the top of the gorge. Lewis viewed the falls on July 16th, 1806.

The ravine located below Crooked Falls is where Clark and his group spent the night of June 17, 1805 as they surveyed the area for their portage.

📍 **Great Falls Lower Portage**, The area is located on private land. Interpretive site is located above the river on Salem Road. View the portage from the W side of the river at Sulphur Springs Belt Creek (see directions below)

On June 13, 1805, Lewis and Clark got their first view of the towering falls of the Missouri River. While the falls were certainly amazing, the corps experience in this area was filled with peril: they ran into bears, mountain lions and several of the expedition were ill. And, they needed to somehow get past these dangerous falls. They had to carry everything overland the 18mile to bypass this obstacle. After floods, mosquitos and carving out two canoes to carry their supplies, the Corps portaged around the falls on July 15. But you can visit the Lewis and Clark National Historical Park (see below) and view a two-story diorama of the falls.

Lewis wrote,

"...whin my ears were saluted with the agreeable sound of a fall of water and advancing a little further; I saw the spray arise above the plain like a collumn of smoke ... which soon began to make a roaring too tremendious to be mistaken for any cause short of the great falls of the Missouri..."

Day Trip

Take in all the water sites in Great Falls, start at the Missouri River and 15th St NE on the S side of the river and turn right (east) on N. River Rd for the first turn off on Giant Springs Rd and stop at the Lewis and Clark Interpretive Center to get oriented and take in views E and W on the river. Continue on Giant Springs Rd to Giant Spring State Park. Your next stop on Giant Springs Rd is Rainbow Falls. Back track to 15th St and cross the Missouri to N. River Rd and turn east to Black Eagle Falls. Back track to 15th St NE and continue N, briefly, to Wire Mills Rd E and turn E on Rainbow Dam Rd to Rainbow Dam. Continue on Rainbow Dam Rd to Ryan Dam where you can walk the swinging bridge over the river. Follow Ryan Dam Rd to Morony Dam Rd N. You'll be moving away from the river here but don't worry the road eventually wraps around and returns to the Missouri at the Morony Reservoir. Sulphur springs is just up the road.

✦ **Morony Dam**, US 87NE to Morony Dam Rd, E, accessible on River's Edge Trail, picnic table

Named after John G Morony, the director of the Montana Power Company the dam opened in1930. The old town site can still be seen above the dam.

🚶 **Sulphur Springs Trail**, 87NE to Morony Dam Rd, E for 11 miles to the Morony Dam town site (now abandoned), 3.6m RT. Map.

Hike the native prairie almost as it was when Lewis arrived here to get Sulphur for a sick Sacagawea in June 1805.

CM Russell Museum, 1498 400 13th St N, 406-727-8787, https://cmrussell.org/, 10-5, closed Mon in summer, closed Mon and Tues the rest of the year. $9 for adults, $4 students.

Russel's western art tends to romanticize the west but also includes an empathetic approach to Native Americans. Paintings of the Lewis and Clark expedition are scattered throughout the museum. Probably the most well-known is "Lewis and Clark Meeting the Flatheads in Ross Hole, September 4, 1805". The painting highlights the importance of the Native Americans in Russell's view of the west. The Indians dominate the foreground while Lewis and Clark are seen off to the right, small figures in the background.

Great Falls Upper Portage Camp and White Bear Island, not open to the public. Interpretive panels at 40th Ave S.

The islands here mark the end of the portage. The men hauled six heavy dugouts and their baggage after walking 18miles of the prairie and encountering multiple white bears. On July 4th, 1805, the men celebrated both the nation's birthday and their own success. In 1806, they returned for their cache on July 13. Grizzly bears were in abundance. From here Lewis took Drouillard, Reubin and Joseph Field to continue up the Marias seeking its northern most point. The remaining groups moved to the Three Forks to await Clark's party. Unfortunately, the area has changed significantly over the last 100 years including the river itself changing its route.

Ryan Island Park Picnic Area and Ryan Dam, part of the Great Falls Portage National Historical Landmark. 160 Ryan Dam Rd., 406-268-2324, https://www.visitmt.com/listings/general/recreation-area/ryan-island-park-picnic-area.html, Park along the road and then take the suspension bridge over to the park.

A lovely park has been built downstream of the Ryan Dam, built in 1915. While the park has wonderful dam views, it also includes a covered picnic area, walking trails and sprawling green lawns. No restroom in the park. The River's Edge Trail connects to Great Falls.

Lewis scaled the cliff on the side of the road on his hike to figure out where the falls were.

From Great Falls West

Vaughn

At the intersection of I15 and US89 on the Sun River, 12m W of Great Falls.

Take a break at **Big Sky Deli** (190 US 89, 406-964-8553) for sandwiches and ice cream. Also a good spot to stop for a cappuccino. Small country store as well (candy for the kids!).

- ⚑ **First Peoples Buffalo Jump State Park**, 342 Ulm-Vaughn Rd, 406-866-2217, Visitor Center open 4/15-9/30 8am-6pm, 10-4pm rest of the year. Park is open daily in summer; weds-sun rest of the year. Picnic tables, restrooms at visitor center and at top of the cliff, 3m RT trail to cliff.

  Visitor center is dedicated to the first peoples and focuses on the different Indian tribes and their use of buffalo and how vital the buffalo were to their survival. The visitor center sits below the jump, and you can walk a loop trail through the prairie up to the jump, a guided tour, or drive up yourself. It's worth it to go with a ranger and hear how the jump functioned and how important the buffalo were to survival. It's easy to imagine how unfair it was to chase a bunch of clueless buffalo off a ridge to their death; but when you hear the guide explain both how difficult the process was and how necessary to survival, it is easier to appreciate why this is such an important destination. Recommended.

  The jump was used for at least 1000 years before Lewis and Clark came through the area on May 29, 1805. Lewis describes the process in his journals:

  "one of the most active and fleet young men is selected and disguised in a robe of buffalo skin ... he places himself at a distance between a herd of buffalo and a precipice proper for the purpose; the other Indians now surround the herd on the back and flanks and at a signal agreed on all show themselves at the same time moving forward towards the buffalo; the disguised Indian or decoy has taken care to place himself sufficiently near the buffalo to be noticed by them when they take to flight and running before them they follow him in full speed to the precipice; the Indian (decoy) in the mean time has taken care to secure himself in some cranny in the cliff... the part of the decoy I am informed is extremely dangerous."

- ⛰ **Square Butte (Fort Mountain)**, visible from I15 and Hwy. 89 SW of Vaughn

  Lewis identified this rock as "Fort Mountain" in July 1805. At some point, the name morphed into Square Butte, though this morphology has not been traced. This "laccolith" was formed by an intrusion of magma pushing through weaker layers of rock to form this 300 foot formation.

Lincoln

MT 200, between Great Falls (86m E) and Missoula (80m W)

Lincoln District Ranger Office 1569 Highway 200, (406) 362-7000, 8-4:30, closed Sat-Sun. You may want to drop into the office just to view the enormous Grizzly in the front lobby.

> Take a break at the **Lincoln Pit Stop** (900 Main St, 406-362-4848, http://www.lincolnpitstop.com/home) for quick fast food. Eat in or take your fish and chips, pizza or burger to go. For something different, get The Harley, a pork chop sandwich. Huckleberry ice cream is a great way to end your meal.

🏛 **Lewis and Clark Pass**, 9m E of Lincoln off MT 200 on Alice Creek Rd (FR 293) 11m (see detailed directions below), 3m RT hiking trail

If you make it to this pass, it's worth it to climb the trail to enjoy the expansive views Lewis and Clark would have viewed. On July 7th, Lewis' party climbed to the top of the pass where they could see Square Butte to the North.

⚐ **Alice Creek Historic District**, To visit Alice Creek Historic District, travel east on Highway 200 from Lincoln, Montana. The turnoff to Alice Creek is 10 miles east of Lincoln. From Highway 200, travel 11 miles north on the well-graded dirt Alice Creek Road #293 to reach the parking area for the Alice Creek Trailhead, the hike to the pass is 1.7 miles of gradual climbing with 750ft elevation gain. Trail leads to Lewis and Clark pass, 406-362-7000. Vault Toilets, picnic tables at trailhead. Interpretive signs.

Alice Creek branches off the Blackfoot River and was recommended as a shortcut to Lewis by the Nez Perce. This is one of the places along the Lewis and Clark trail where you can almost step back in time to 1806. On July 7, they passed through the Alice Creek drainage. With few roads or other evidence of civilization, Alice Creek remains largely as it was when the Corps set up their camp. If you look closely, you can see signs of the Cokahlarishkit Trail (also known as The Road to the Buffalo), the Native American trail that Lewis and his detachment followed. Rock cairns and travois ruts are still present. Some parts of the area are on private land.

Ovando

Highway 200, E of Missoula

🏛 **Lewis Minus Clark Expedition interpretation kiosk**, MT 200

On July 6, 1806, Lewis with his group camped near Ovando at the confluence of the Big Blackfoot River and a creek.

Bonner

Hwy. 200 E of Missoula

Historical Signs on Hwy. 200

Three historical signs provide interpretation of area history, one of these focuses on Lewis' homeward journey.

    🏛 **Bonner Milltown History Center & Museum**, 9397 Hwy. 200, Bonner post office, 406-258-6335 (call to arrange a visit), http://www.bonnermilltownhistory.org/about/history-center-news/, 9:30-11:30 Tues, 2-4:30 Weds-Thurs

    Community generated museum. Stop in and ask about Meriwether Lewis' stop in the area on July 5th on the Road to the Buffalo.

Missoula

Glacier Lake Missoula

The geology that Lewis and Clark encountered and that we still see today is a result of Glacier Lake Missoula, and you'll hear and read about this phenomenon at almost any interpretive or visitor center or museum in the area. About one million years ago, glaciers came down and blocked the Clark river outlet creating pressure that builds to the extent that it breaks the ice and a flood bursts forward containing more than 500 cubic miles of water that burst out of the break at 10 times the combined flow of all the rivers in the world. The water rushes out leaving rocks behind it. The largest rocks are carried the furthest, and you can see these outlying boulders miles away. They are called, glacier erratics. This process happened over and over again, at least dozens of times, for 2500 years.

Lewis and his small group of ten men and five guides camped here on July 3, 1806.

Missoula Walk-In Visitor Center, 101 East Main, 800-526-3465, http://destinationmissoula.org/.

* **Montana Museum of Art and Culture**, 32 Campus Dr, 406-243-2019, https://www.umt.edu/montanamuseum/, hours vary, see website or call

  Wide ranging permanent collection that includes contemporary Native art.

* **Fort Missoula Historical Museum**, 3400 Captain Rawn Way, 406-728-3476, http://fortmissoulamuseum.org/, 10-5pm, opens noon on Sun.

  Stroll the grounds and view the many historical buildings dating from the late 19th century to the early 20th. The museum also includes historic exhibits and art.

* **National Museum of Forest Services**, 6305 Hwy. 10W, 406-541-6374, https://forestservicemuseum.org/, 10-4 Summer

  The archive includes over 50,000 historical artifacts mostly from the 20th century, but the visitor center highlights only a few of these at any given time. The focus is on forest service related activities like smokejumpers and conservationists.

* **Missoula Art Museum**, 335 N Pattee St, 406-728-0447, http://www.missoulaartmuseum.org/, 10-5 Tues-Sat.

  Focus on contemporary art related to the region and state.

* **Montana Natural History Center**, 120 Hickory St, #A, 406-327-0405, http://www.montananaturalist.org/, $3 adults, $1 kids.

  Flora, fauna and natural history of western Montana. This is a great museum especially for kids. While the exhibits are not focused on Lewis and Clark, the Glacial Lake Missoula exhibit is helpful in understanding Montana geology that Lewis and Clark encountered.

* **Milltown State Park**, 1353 Deer Creek Rd, 406-542-5533, day use, vault toilets, trails, bird watching, picnic areas, storyboard, Map.

  The newest park in the Montana State park system, the park provides an interpretive plaza that explains both the geology of the area and its history including Lewis and Seaman's 4th of July, 1806 visit. The park restores the confluence of the Clark Fork and Blackfoot Rivers. Milltown bridge and heritage trail

+ **Smokejumper Visitor Center**, 5765 W Broadway, 406-329-4934, 8:30-5 summer, winter call ahead.

    Interactive exhibits and tour of the facility.

Pablo
60m N of US93 from Missoula

+ **The People's Center**, 56633 Hwy 93, 406-675-0160, http://www.peoplescenter.org/, 8am-5pm, closed Sun, $5 adults

    The Salish, Kootenai and Pend d'Oreille are the focus of this cultural center. The Salish interacted with Lewis and Clark. Tours available and highly recommended.

From Great Falls South

Cascade
I15 S 27m from Great Falls. The Missouri River runs along the E side of town.

+ **Tower Rock State Park**, 2325 Old US Hwy. 91, Cascade, W side of the Missouri River, 8m S of Cascade at I15, interpretive panels, .5m one-way hiking trail to tower rock, vault toilets

    The large rock formation at 424 feet marks the transition from prairie to Rocky Mountains. Lewis helped to name this place, writing in his journal

    "At this place there is a large rock of 400 ft. high which stands immediately in the gap which the Missouri makes on its passage from the mountains... This rock I called the tower. It may be ascended with some difficulty nearly to its summit and from there is a most pleasing view of the country we now are about to leave."

Helena
Helena is several miles W of the Missouri river and Lewis and Clark never came through the city proper. But they did pass through S at Townsend and N at Gates of the Mountain (see below).

The Capitol of Montana, Helena combines an industrial surrounds with a lovely downtown and capitol building. The area had enormous wealth in the 19th and early 20th century as a result of the copper mining. There are many mansions throughout the city, and the city is diverse because of the mining workers. There is a beautiful mosque and a lovely Cathedral built in 1914. If you get a chance, walk through the State Capitol building and check out the art.

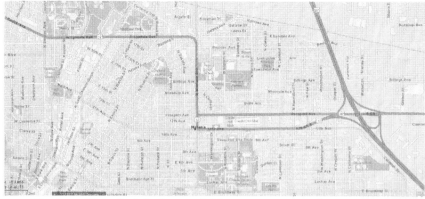

★ **Montana Historical Society and Museum**, 225 N Roberts, 406-444-2694, https://mhs.mt.gov/, 9-5, closed Sun, $5 adult, $1 child.

Large historical and cultural collection with 50,000 artifacts. A variety of art pieces depict the expedition.

🏛 **Great Northern Town Center**, 40 W 14th St, between Getchell St and Lyndale Ave East., 406-457-5542,

This was not a place Lewis and Clark visited, but an interpretive trail represents their journey. You can stroll the trail and experience some of their passage through running water, climbable rocks and other trail markers. The path includes 19 historical sites with interpretive signage. It's a good place to stop if you are planning on visiting some of the "real" places, especially if you've got kids with you. And you can grab an ice cream and ride the carousel while you are there!

⚓ **Gates of the Mountains**, 3131 Gates of the Mountains, I 15N from Helena for 15m to Gates of the Mountains Rd E, 406-458-5241, http://www.gatesofthemountains.com/, 2 hour guided tour boat, $16 adult, $10 child, Reserve online.

This area remains largely unchanged from when Lewis and Clark ventured through. The water level has increased 15feet as a result of the dams, but the scenery itself has changed little. If you take the boat ride up the river, you'll see sedimentary and sandstone cliffs, the results of fires, eagles, osprey and their nests, cormorants, mountain goats, fir trees and pines. The cliffs are 5 1/4m in length and 1000 ft above the water. The area was shaped by the Missouri River starting around 3 million years ago. Guides interpret the landscape as they guide their boat up the river. This is one of the best water routes to see the Lewis and Clark river.

Meriwether Picnic Area, boat access, picnic tables, toilets, access to the Meriwether Canyon trail. The Picnic area is where the Corps of Discovery camped on July 19, 1805.

On July 19, 1805 the corps came through the towering rock formations that make up Gates of the Mountains and stared in awe at the 1200ft high limestone cliffs as Lewis wrote, I shall call this place: "GATES OF THE MOUNTAINS".

Townsend

SE of Helena on US 287 about 35 miles. The Missouri River runs along the W side of town and into

📖 **Broadwater School and Community Library**, 201 N Spruce St, 406-266-5060, 2-7 Mon-Fri, 9-3 Sat, closed Sun, informative Lewis and Clark section.

♀ **Crimson Bluffs**, http://www.crimsonbluffs.org/, 43 mile self-guided auto tour,

Lewis described these red-hued cliffs in the journal on July 24, 1805. The bluffs have been preserved almost as they were when Lewis and Clark viewed them.

Tour the Crimson Bluffs, using the auto tour link above, begins at 415 S Front St. Much of the river road is gravel. Interpretive sign on the left side of River Rd. The best time to view the bluffs is early morning, mid-summer.

📖 **Broadwater County Museum**, 133 N. Walnut, 406-266-5252, May 15-Sept 15 1-5,

Lewis and Clark exhibit includes a replica dugout canoe, maps and photographs as well as a map of the Crimson Cliffs self-guided auto tour.

📖 **Yorks Islands**, S of Townsend off River Rd, take US 287 N to Indian Creek/River Rd W (you can use "F" on the self-guided auto tour under Crimson Bluffs above), 406-994-4042, boat launch, picnic tables, fishing, camping, toilets, River Rd interpretive sign

Lewis and Clark named these islands "York's 8 Islands".

Take a break at the **Mountie Moose Bakery** (109 E Broadway, 406-266-5800) with a cup of coffee and a cookie. Or stop for breakfast or lunch.Or, head up US 287/12 to **Flamingo Grill**

(80 Silso Rd, 406-266-3990) for a unique and tasty dining experience. The Flamingo is a little trailer serving sandwiches, ice cream and salads from a window. Picnic tables available.

Canyon Ferry

Take US 12 E from Townsend to MT 284 N and up along the E side of the Missouri River

🏕 **Canyon Ferry**, 7700 Canyon Ferry Rd, 406-475-3310, boating, camping, fishing, picnicking, hunting, nature study, swimming. There are three marina concessions (Goose Bay Marina, Kim's Marina and yacht Basin Marina) with full services, Map

Lewis and Clark set up nine campsites along this area between July 21-25. The sites were located near Canyon ferry dam, Beaver Creek, and an area near Dry Creek S of Townsend. They note in the journal the terrible clouds of mosquitos and gnats that tormented them. Our earliest record of wildlife species in the area come from the journals.

Toston

S of Townsend

🏕 **Toston Dam**, US 287 S from Townsend to Toston Dam Rd, camping, picnic tables, toilets, interpretive sign

On July 25th, 1805 the corps camped on the W side of the Missouri just up from Toston Dam. The area below the dam is The Gates of the Mountain (see above).

Three Forks

Off I90, exit 278

It is here in Three Forks in July 1805 where Sacagawea was reunited with her brother, and perhaps more importantly for the expedition, it's where Lewis and Clark make contact

with the Shoshone and get the horses they need. And the town itself is named after the three forks of the river that come together, the Jefferson, Madison and Gallatin.

Lewis wrote in July 1805, *"[i]f we do not find [the Shoshoni] or some other nation who have horses I fear the successfull issue of our voyage will be very doubtfull."*

Take a break at the **Wheat Montana Farms Bakery & Deli** (10778 US 87, 406-285-3614) for coffee and any of the baked goods. But go to **Pompey's grill** (5 N Main St, in the Sacagawea Hotel, 406-285-6515) for dinner. This is a surprising gem with tasty, tasteful dishes.

Take a break in the **Sacajawea Hotel**, 5 North Main, 406-285-6515, https://www.sacajaweahotel.com/rooms/sacajawea/) refurbished in 2010, and enjoy Western Hospitality in a truly authentic 1910 white clapboard setting. The rooms are all named after expedition members but all are luxurious. The Shoshone are the simplest, the Charbonneau suites the most luxurious and the cabins the most spacious. But my personal favorite is the John Colter with its small sitting area.

- **Missouri Headwaters Heritage Museum**, 202 S Main St, 406-285-4778, http://www.tfhistory.org/, June 1-Sept 30 9-5, 11-3 Sunday. Call for hours off-season.

  Very eclectic selection of artifacts, with a few significant Lewis and Clark items including a dugout canoe used in a Lewis and Clark documentary.

- **Missouri Headwaters State Park**, 1585 Trident Rd., take the Frontage rd./MT2 along I90 E to Trident Rd N, 406-285-3610, Park includes hiking, 4-mile biking path, camping, restrooms, picnic shelter, and a junior ranger program. Map. Camp where Lewis and Clark once camped. Interpretive signs.

  Here, the Jefferson, Madison and Gallatin Rivers come together. The river confluence was an important gathering spot for Native Americans for centuries and continued to be a meeting point for trappers and settlers. Note the hill down the road from the old Gallatin City hotel; here is where Lewis stood to scan the expansive valley.

  The Corps reached this uncharted river intersection on July 25, 1805 after traveling 2500 miles from the Mississippi. Lewis camped here for three nights to take celestial observations. They named the three rivers in honor of Jefferson and two of his cabinet members, Madison and Gallatin. But the more important issue was determining which of these three rivers to follow. Knowing that the Shoshone also used this area, they hoped to encounter them for some guidance on their travel. They selected the southwest flowing tributary, what they had named The Jefferson. At this point in the expedition, there was still hope that they would locate that mythical river that would take them to the Pacific.

The men continued to look for a point from which they would be able to see the rivers flowing to the Pacific.

Lewis climbed on Lewis Rock, a limestone cliff, to get a view of the rivers and the surrounding area on July 26th 1805. From here, he could clearly see the Gallatin, Jefferson and Madison rivers. Between the rivers he identified "Fort Rock", a limestone outcrop with a flat top where he observed would be a good place for a fort.

- **Lewis and Clark Caverns State Park**, 25 Lewis and Clark Caverns Rd, I90 W to exit 256, MT2 E 406-287-3541, visitor center, camping, cabins, interpretive programs, 6.3m loop trail, May 1-Sept. 30, 8:30-4:30daily, until 6:30 in mid-summer. Map.

  While the corps never visited the caverns, as far as we know, they did come in sight of them on July 31, 1805. A two-hour guided tour travels two miles in the walkable cave or take one of the other hikes.

Take a break on your way to The Caverns at **Lahood Park steakhouse** (960 MT2, 406-287-3281, http://www.lahoodpark.com/), it's worth the drive. Hand-cut, char broiled steaks served for dinner. A nearby sign explains the Lewis and Clark expedition passing through here on Aug 1, 1805.

- **Madison Buffalo Jump**, 6990 Buffalo Jump Rd, I90 exit at Logan S on Buffalo Jump Rd, 406-285-3610, vault toilets, picnic areas, hiking, interpretive signs. Map.

  The jump has been used for 2000 years to stampede the buffalo herds over a massive cliff.

- **Headwater Trail**, trail access on Trident Rd, 4th Ave E in Three Forks or Droulliard Fishing Access on MT 2, paved network of trails that goes through Three Forks to Missouri Headwaters State Park.

Whitehall
I90 W 30 miles from Three Forks.
- **Whitehall Lewis & Clark Murals**, throughout the downtown.

  Bicentennial murals depict the expedition. 12 were created but only 10 remain. They trace the Corps trip up the Jefferson River in 1805 to the Corps' return in 1806. Local artist Kit Mather did the murals.

Take a break at the **Pepper Tree Deli** (105 W Legion, 406-287-9870) and enjoy a house-made sandwich made while you wait or a Caesar Salad. Ice cream is also available.

Butte

W of Whitehall on I90 about 30 miles.

- **Two Camps Vista**, 106 North Parkmont, exit 193 off I15, 406-458-4744, $5 day use

  With expansive views over the Missouri, Two Camps recognizes Lewis and Clark's camp nearby on July 20, 1805

- **Clark's Bay Day Use Site/Devil's Elbow**, 106 North Parkmont, 406-533-7600, restrooms, picnic tables, trails, swimming, boat launch, interpretive display.

  Amazing views of the mountains and on Hauser Lake.

- **Mai Wah Museum**, 17 W Mercury St, 406-723-3231, http://www.maiwah.org/, 10-4pm, Closed Sun-Mon, open in summer but call year round, $5 adult, $3 children

  Museum is dedicated to interpreting Asian history in the West.

- **Lexington Stamp Mill Gardens**, 2001 Porter, corner of Granite and Arizona, 406-723-6656, restrooms, picnic tables, free

  Botanical gardens and an historic stamp mill.

- **Montana Tech Mineral Museum**, 1300 W Park St in the Montana Tech Library, 406-496-4414, 9-5, free, http://www.mbmg.mtech.edu/museum/museum.html,

  Rocks and Minerals from all over the world including space.

- **World Museum of Mining**, 155 Museum Way, 406-723-7211, http://miningmuseum.org/, 9-6 from April-Oct with daily tours. Reserve online, $8.50 adults, $5 students, tours extra.

    History of mining and tours of various types of mines.

Twin Bridges

S of Whitehall on MT 55 S to MT 41S, 27 miles.

Lewis and Clark camped near the Beaverhead River.

- **Madison County Lewis & Clark Interpretive Park**, 2 Fairgrounds Loop off MT41/W4th Ave, 406-684-5824, picnic tables, interpretive signs.

    In August 1805, Lewis and Clark traveled up the Jefferson River to the confluence of four rivers, the Jefferson, Beaverhead, Big Hole and Ruby all near the present day Twin Bridges. And, just south of Twin Bridges, Sacagawea recognized the area as the Shoshone homeland. A 6-foot bronze statue of Sacagawea, Pomp and Seaman dominates the park.

- **Beaverhead Rock State Park**, 62 Beaverhead Rock Rd, 5m SW of Twin Bridges, 406-834-3413, trail, interpretive sign.

    Beaverhead Rock stands 380ft above the river, 230ft higher than Clark estimated. It is made of limestone, deposited 325 million years ago, like nearby Gates of the Mountains.

    The rock was a well-known landmark for Native Americans of the area. On August 8, 1805, Sacagawea recognized this rock as the location where she had been kidnapped several years earlier. In Shoshone, she indicated the rock was called beaverhead because of its resemblance to that creature. Recognizing the rock gave the Corps some hope that soon they would connect with the Shoshone people themselves. Lewis and a small advance party including Drouillard, John Shields and Hugh McNeal were sent out to attempt to locate the Indians while Clark continued down the river.

- **The Big Hole River**, runs from Wisdom N to Twin Bridges along MT43, blue trout fishing

    Lewis and Clark located the Big Hole, what they called The Wisdom, at the headwaters of the Jefferson River at Twin Bridges.

Bannack

S of Twin Bridges on MT 41-S and MT 278 W to Bannack Bench Rd to Hendricks Mill Rd, 54miles.

+ **Bannack State Park**, 721 Bannack Rd, 8-9 summer, 8-5 winter, visitor center 10-6 summer, $6, camping, skating in winter.

    Gold rush in Montana is recreated in this state park with its ghost town main street.

Wisdom

From Bannack, Wisdom is about 50m N on MT 278W

+ **The Big Hole National Battlefield**, 16425 Hwy. 43 W, Hwy 43 10m W of Wisdom, 406-689-3155, https://www.nps.gov/biho/index.htm, visitor center, film, four trails

    Commemorates the battle between the Nez Perce and the Army on Aug 9-10, 1877. On July 6th, 1806, Clark's group camped a few miles W of the battlefield.

Take a break at **The Crossing Bar and Grill** (327 County Rd, 406-689-3260) for homemade soups and sandwiches or burgers. Full breakfasts.

Dillon Area

On I15 and MT 41. Good place to set up a base camp.

Dillon Visitor Information Center, 10 W Reeder St, 406-683-5511

+ **Clark Canyon Reservoir and Camp Fortunate**, 1100 Hwy. 41, 20m S of Dillon off I15, 406-683-6472.

    On August 13, 1805, Lewis met up with several Indians on horseback, one of which happened to be Sacagawea's brother. Through all kinds of promises, Lewis was able to persuade the Shoshone to wait with him for Clark who finally arrived on Aug 17th. The meeting was "fortunate" for the corps who had been hoping to meet up with Shoshone for some time, hence the name of the area. On August 20, 1805, the corps buried one of their Caches here which they retrieved on July 8, 1806.

    The building of the dam drowned Camp Fortunate, but today there are interpretive signs at the site and a dugout canoe like the one used by Lewis and Clark. Note that these signs focus on Sacagawea's contribution to the corps.

Take a break in Dillon where there are several good choices. Try **La Fiesta Mexicana** (510 N Montana St, 406-660-0915) a "food bus" for fast, tasty Mexican with limited outdoor seating. **The Atlantic Street Mercantile** (435 S Atlantic St, 406-988-0711) is a fun, lively place with burgers, hot dogs, ice cream and really good breakfast. Also a good pace for an espresso. Be sure to get hashbrowns and something with chile verde. **Sparky's** (420 E Poindexter St, 406-683-2828) is a sit down place for dinner with a large decent menu, tvs for the game, and local brewed ale. If you have time to spend the night (and don't want a chain), the best lodging is the Fly Shop Inn (406-683-3462, https://backcountryangler.com/dillon-montana-lodging/) , a three unit bed and breakfast in Dillon. Comfortable, spacious rooms with Montana décor.

- 🏛 **Beaverhead County Museum**, 15 S Montana St, 406-683-5027, $3 adult, free for children under 12

  Homesteader's cabin, pioneer artifacts and a Lewis and Clark diorama. Museum is in the restored Dillon Depot.

- 🏛 **Clark's Lookout State Park**, one mile N of Dillon off old state Hwy. 91, turning W on Lovers Leap Rd, 406-834-3414, picnic area, interpretive signs, short hike to lookout.

  After Lewis and his small advance party set out over land to locate the Shoshone, Clark and the rest of the Corps continued down the river. On Aug 13, 1805 Clark ascended this rock where he made a map of the area, and the map is on one of the interpretive panels. Lewis' party encountered several Shoshone girls and a woman. The girls fled but the woman stayed. After some efforts, Lewis was able to convince her he was friendly, and through them the party was able to finally make contact with the Shoshone and Chief Cameahwait.

  If you stand at the lookout, you will see a decidedly different landscape than the one Clark viewed and mapped. The Utah and Northern railroad tracks and the small town of Dillon are visible.

Idaho

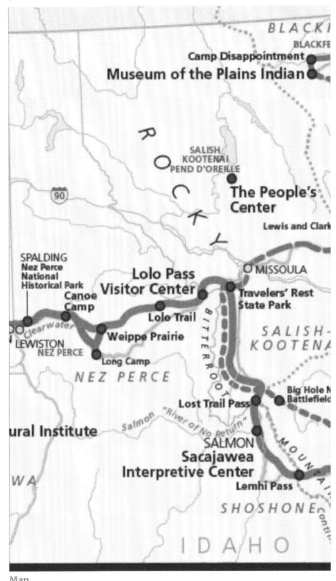

Map

Lewis, accompanied by three of his men, reconnoitered the area that is now Idaho ahead of the rest of the Corps on August 12, 1805. Their hope was to find horses to continue the expedition because they could go no further on the Missouri. Luckily, they were successful. It was not lucky, however, to discover the range after range of mountains that loomed in their way. After significant struggles, they finally headed out of Idaho around Oct 8th, 1805 into Washington. They returned on May 5th, 1806, meeting up with the Nez Perce. They had to retreat after their first attempt to cross the Bitterroots; the weather was just to bad. They stayed with the Nez Perce for another month before they were able to make any progress. While this was a long wait, it was one of the most profitable for gathering plant specimens during the entire expedition. Lewis collected at least ¼ of his plants during this layover. They finally departed Idaho for good on June 29th, 1806.

Float trips in Idaho that focus on the Lewis and Clark Expedition.

Rawhide Outfitters, 208-756-4276, http://rawhideoutfitters.com/activities/lewis-clark-tours/, Offers a variety of tours of Lewis and Clark sites in Idaho.

Tendoy

Tendoy is a crossroads on Hwy. 28, just over the Lemhi pass. The area was named for the head chief of the Lemhi Shoshone from 1863-1907. There is a small store but no other services.

From Aug 12-20th 1805, the corps stayed in this area at various places.

- **Lemhi Pass**, 12m E of Tendoy off ID 28, on unpaved FR 013 (Agency Creek Rd), Elevation 7339ft

   Lewis, George Drouillard, John Shields and Hugh McNeal made up the advance party seeking the Shoshone and the potential horses they might be able to provide the group to traverse the mountains. They crossed the Continental Divide and the 2 mile Lemhi Pass, which now borders Idaho and Montana, on August 12th 1805. The party used an Indian hunting trail to traverse the pass. Here was their first encounter with the Columbia River as well, as they drew water from the head of Agency Creek, a tributary of the Columbia.

   The landscape today is very much like it was in 1805. The sagebrush and bunch grasses and the fir and pines are all native plants. Elk and deer are often seen, just as Lewis and Clark might have seen them. And look to the west to see the view of the Rockies that the corps would have seen. Imagine what it might have been like to look out over that range and know you are going to have to cross it on foot, boat and horse, if you are lucky. Needless to say, Lewis realized at this point the rest of the journey was not going to be an easy flow down a river.

   Interpretive Sign at the pass highlights Drouillard's interpretive skills as he uses sign language to communicate with the Shoshoni.

   Guided Horseback Riding is offered by Rawhide Outfitters, 208-756-4276, http://rawhideoutfitters.com/activities/lewis-clark-tours/.

- **Lewis and Clark Backcountry Byway**, this is a true "backcountry" route and should be treated with some caution. It includes Lemhi pass above. The gravel road is accessible to passenger cars but it's a good idea to make sure you've got water and a spare tire along with you as you traverse the 39 mile route. Interpretive signs along the route add historic context. This is an excellent opportunity to experience the natural world that Lewis and Clark traversed, including opportunities to see birds, plants and animals that they saw. Start at the tour kiosk at the beginning of the loop at mm 3.7 on Idaho 28. The full drive will take 3 hours. Restrooms are located at mm26. Route Guide. Birding Guide

Warm Springs Rd, 3.0 turn off here for Backcountry Byway

Meeting of Two cultures, 4.1m on Back Country Byway, .4m on Alkali Flat Rd, sign and hiking activities.

First Flag Unfurling Site, MM8.2, an interpretive sign marks the spot where Lewis first unfurled an American flag on Aug 31, 1805 after crossing the Continental Divide. Just up the road at MM 120.5 is the site of "Upper Village" where the advance party stayed after meeting the Shoshone. The site is on private property but an interpretive sign along the road explains its significance.

Pattee Creek Overlook, MM 9.6, Clark camped at the creek on Aug 19, 1805

Lemhi Pass, MM 24 (see separate listing)

Sacajawea Memorial Camp, .2m on Montana Side, camping, toilets, picnic tables, interpretive signs, wildflower trail. The interpretive sign for the camp is actually located N of the site itself. Here Lewis paused and wrote in his journal.

Horseshoe Bend Creek, MM 25, the men drank from this creek where it joins Agency Creek.

Agency Creek Campground, MM 31.5, interpretive signs, toilets, camping. Road is steep.

Salmon Idaho

This area of Idaho where US93 and ID28 intersect was once the base for Shoshone, and Lewis and Clark stopped in this area on their trip.

BLM Salmon Field Office, 1206 S Challis St, Route 2, 208-756-5400. 7:45-4:30, closed Sat-Sun.

   📖 **Sacajawea Interpretive and Cultural Center**, 2700 Main St, 208-756-1188, http://www.sacajaweacenter.org/, Memorial Day-Labor Day or by appointment, 8-5, Sun 12:30-5, $5 per person, $12 per family. Museum, trails. Center is located in a city park which is open year round. Birding Guide

     The 70 acre park focuses on Sacagawea and her participation in the Lewis and Clark journey. Regular programs and events are offered during the day and evening hours. Check the website for the current schedule. The events include tours, talks on historical figures and field trips. Demonstrations take place in the village on Thursday and Saturday. Classes are offered to make a variety of traditional crafts and tools including felt bags, beading and flint knives. Check out the life-size Seaman statue and the Sacagawea monument with Pomp. Highly recommended.

> Take a break at the **Shady Nook** (501 Riverfront Dr, 208-756-4182) and sit outdoors while you enjoy a burger and fries. Very upscale for dinner. **Bertram's Brewery** (101 S Andrews St, 208-756-3391) is a great place for a Reuben and a beer. And make sure you stop at **Oddfellows** (510 Main St, 208-756-1122) for coffee and a croissant. It's also a good place to just hang out and relax.

   ✦ **Lemhi County Historical Society**, 210 Main St, 208-756-3342, http://www.lemhicountymuseum.org/, 10-4, $2, children under 12 free.

     Offers large variety of events throughout the year from discussions to poetry readings. The museum's focus is the Lemhi Shoshone artifacts which includes clothing, beadwork, and art. Mining and ranching exhibits are also included.

The Lemhi-Shoshone played an important role in the Lewis and Clark expedition. In addition to the guidance and interpretive role of Sacajawea, they also provided horses, food and a guide, Old Toby, to take them through the mountains. It is arguable whether the expedition would have been successful without the help of the Lemhi-Shoshone. Evidence suggests that ancestors of the Lemhi Shoshone came to this area as long as 12,000 years ago. Like many tribes of the west, the Shoshone suffered greatly once the area was settled by Europeans. To read more about their history and struggles, check out this webpage.

- **Discovery Hill**, 1m N of Salmon via North St. Scenic overlook, interpretive signs, toilets, trailhead.

  Over 200 years ago, Lewis and Clark crossed over this hill but as recently as 40 years ago, the place had become the town dump. Today, the hill has been returned to its original state, or at least as close to that as possible. And a 1.6m discovery hill podcast has been produced to complement a visit to the hill and includes information about Lewis and Clark.

Take a break and stay the night in the **Syringa Lodge** (13 Gott Lane, 208-756-4424, http://www.syringalodge.com/) which has great views from its many decks, unique décor and a huge fireplace for gathering. Breakfast is included. Rooms are upscale with fine furnishings.

North Fork Area

Full Services are available at this tiny "fork" in the road at the intersection of the North Fork and The Salmon River on US 93.

North Fork Ranger Station, 11 Casey Rd, 208-865-2700, 8-4:30pm, closed Sat-Sun.

- **Tower Rock Campground**, Hwy 93, S of North Fork, 208-756-5400, camping, restrooms, interpretive signs, picnic tables, boat launch, fishing.

  On August 21 and 25th, Clark and his party camped near this spot as they checked out the Salmon River. Note the pyramid like rocks further up the road at MM 315.7. Here Clark noted that they "passed remarkable rock resembling pirimids on the left side". Interpretive panels explain geology of Tower Rock and Clark's campsite.

- **Wagonhammer Springs picnic area**, MM 324.4, Hwy. 93 S of North Fork, picnic and toilet facilities,

  Walk two miles up Wagonhammer creek to follow Clark's path to the mouth of Thompson Gulch where this is a marked 6 mile trail. Lewis and Clark National Historic Trail, begins at Wagonhammer trailhead, 9.1m for equestrians and hikers.

Gibbonsville

MM 337.2 Hwy. 93 includes food and services. When Lewis and Clark came through this area Sept 1-3, 1805 they were forced to cut a road through some very steep areas that resulted in horses falling down the hillsides, though none were killed.

🏛 **Gibbons Pass**, FR 106, interpretive signs.

> After Clark and Lewis divided up their group at Travelers Rest on July 3, 1806, Clark headed up through the Bitterroot river valley traveling through what is now Gibbons Pass. The pass was later named "Gibbons" after a Colonel in the Nez Perce War.

🏛 **Ravalli County Museum**, 205 Bedford St, Hamilton MT, 406-363-3338, http://ravallimuseum.org/, 10-4 Tues, Weds, Fri, 10-8 Thurs, 9-1 Sat. Free on Thurs and Sat. $3 adults, $1 students.

> Exhibits focus on art, local history and natural history. One exhibit focuses on Lewis and Clarks travels in the bitterroot valley and the Salish tribe. Good local museum. Worth a visit if you are in the area.

> Take a break and have some fun at the **Broken Arrow Resort** (208-865-2241, http://thebrokenarrow.com/), far from fancy, this is a down-home kind of place with occasional live music, rustic cabins and good Mexican food. Lots of great outdoor, hangout areas.

Sula MT

From Tendoy, Sula is directly N on US93

Here, the corps met a band of friendly Salish Indians on September 4th, 1805. Exactly how the corps traveled through this area and where they crossed is contested. But, the journals suggest it was a very rugged and difficult path. An interpretive panel explains the confusion on FR 081 near US93.

🏛 **Sula Ranger Station**, 7338 Hwy. 93S, MM11 Hwy. 93, 406-821-3913, just S of the Salish Village where the expedition spent two nights. Clark camped nearby in July 1806. This ranger station has closed to walk-in visitors.

✦ **Indian Trees Campground**, 7338 Hwy. 93, MM 8 on Hyw. 93, 1 m SW on Forest Rd 729, 406-821-3913, 4820 ft elevation, hiking trails including the Nez Perce National Historic Trail, camping, picnic area, restrooms.

> Named after the scarred trees once carved by Salish, Kootenai, Nez Perce and Shoshoni peoples for the tree's sweet cambium layer. Wagon ruts from early explorers are also visible on the trail.

☖ **Nex Perce Nat'l Historical Trail**, MM7, Hwy. 93 S, to the turnoff for the Indian trees campground (see above), 3.1m

Follow the Nez Perce route during the war of 1877. Hike where Lewis and Clark traveled and get an idea of just how rugged this area is and was. Map. Brochure.

✦ **Lost Trail Pass**, ½ m west of the Continental Divide on Hwy. 93, 13m S of Sula, turn east at MT 43, 406-821-3201, Elevation 7014ft, visitor center, restrooms, interpretive sign at 351.1 Hwy. 93 explains the historical trails in the area.

☖ **Ross Hole**, Hwy 93 next to the Sula County Store (see below), interpretive signs

After leaving Lost Trail Pass on Sept. 4, the corps descended into a small flat valley that was later named Ross Hole. Around 500 Salish Indians (also called Flathead) were camped in the area. They spent the night and shared food with the Salish and departed on Sept. 6th. (One of Charles M Russell's most famous paintings depicts this meeting: Lewis and Clark meet the Indians at Ross' Hole. The painting can be viewed at the Montana State Capitol or here).

Ordway wrote, "*when our officers went to their lodges they gave them each a white robe of dressed skins, and spread them over their Shoulders and put their arms around our necks instead of Shakeing hands as that is their way they appeared glad to See us. they Smoaked with us, then gave us a pleanty Such as they had to eat...*"

> Take a break: **Sula Country Store**, 7060 Hwy. 93 S, 406-821-3364, serves breakfast and lunch in a pretty deserted area. Grocery items are also available.

Darby

Darby is located 17m up US 93 from Sula.

South Valley Visitor Center, 101 East Tanner Ave, 406-821-3753, 12-4:30 Mon-Fri.

☖ **Sacajawea Rest Pocket Park**, 406-531-4172

The little park has picnic tables and a bronze statue of Sacajawea carrying Pomp.

> Take a break at **The Darby** (4485 Thorning Loop, 406-821-0076, http://thedarbybandb.com/). It doesn't get much more remote than this bed and breakfast, but it's a great place to pause and relax for a day or two. Gourmet bed and breakfasts, beautiful outdoor grounds, Japanese soaking grounds, and comfortable rooms. For lunch or dinner, drive into Darby and try **The Blue Joint** (119 N Main St, 406-821-0023, http://www.littlebluejoint.com/) for pizza, fish and chips, or steak and seafood.

Lolo Area

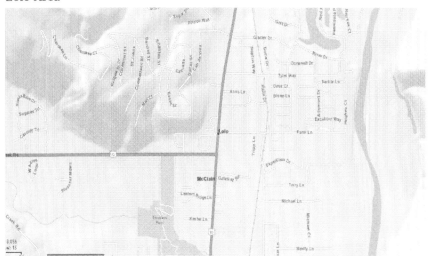

♥ **Travelers Rest State Park**, 6717 Hwy. 12, off Hwy 93 one mile S of Lolo. Visitor Center, restrooms, trails and interpretive panels. Accessible by bike or walking on paved trail.

The Corps had been unable to find a water route from their recent stay in the Shoshone village and paused here on Sept 9, 1805 to take inventory of their plans before they set out over the rugged Lolo Trail. The Corps also camped here on their return trip before Lewis and Clark would split up to do some exploring. Clark departed on July 3, 1806 with his party of 23 men headed toward Beaverhead country. Lewis, with a ten man detachment and Indian guides went North down the Bitterroot River.

Travelers rest is one of the only verified spots along the Lewis and Clark trail. The area used to located 1.5m away but after extensive research, the current location was verified.

The visitor center has tables devoted to the different artifacts of the Lewis and Clark expedition including what they cooked with, their measuring instruments, what they wore and what they used for hunting. In addition, there are exhibits on pioneers and the Salish tribes.

The trails wind through the woods, over a creek and to the verification site.

Verification of Sites

The verification is an interesting story because it shows how Lewis and Clark even today require collaborations between the Anglo-American and Native American Communities. Researchers worked with the Salish tribes to verify this site. The Salish do not appreciate or approve of archaeological digging of Native American history and culture sites. And before Lewis and Clark, Native Peoples used this area for over 2000 years as a gathering place. In order to respect the Native American concerns, scientists used largely non-invasive strategies to examine the area. They were looking for signs of a latrine with evidence of mercury. The mercury was present in some of the medicine that Lewis had brought along in Doctor Benjamen Rush's cure for everything, and it was present in the syringes Lewis used to treat syphilis, of which at least three men were being treated. Locating mercury in the soil would verify that Lewis and Clark had used a certain campsite. This verification allowed for a low-impact archaeological expedition that did not violate the Native People's concerns for disturbing their sacred ground.

🏕 **Packer Meadows**, 1m E of Lolo Pass Visitor Center on Forest Rd 273, camping, interpretive sign. The corps passed through on Sept 13, 1805 and they returned to the meadow on June 29, 1806. If you can get here in mid -late June, you may be able to see the Camas blooms, which cover the area in a blue carpet.

Lewis wrote

"at noon we arrived at the quawmas flatts on the Creek of the same name and halted to graize our horses and dine having traveled 12 miles. we passed our encampment of the of September at 10 ms. where we halted there is a pretty little plain of about 50 acres plentifully stocked with quawmash and from apperances this fromes one of the principal stages or encampments of the indians who pass the mountains on this road."

Take a break at the **Lolo Creek Steakhouse** (6600 US 12, 406-273-2622, https://www.lolocreeksteakhouse.com/Welcome) for a wood-fired steak in a western themed dining room. Across from the steakhouse is Traveler's rest, so you'll be eating in site of a Lewis and Clark campsite!

★ **Lolo Pass Visitor Center**, Hwy. 12 at the ID/MT border, 208-942-3113, https://www.fs.usda.gov/detail/r1/specialplaces/?cid=stelprdb5108516, 5235 ft elevation, restrooms, covered picnic area, 1/4m nature trail, longer trail access, coffee, teas, overhead relief map, lots of brochures and maps, history interpretive panels which include a Lewis and Clark panel.

Highly recommend a stop here. Even in the cold, rain or snow, if it's open it's worth exploring. I recommend taking the nature trail (there may be snow into late May), but the trail is paved and easy, wrapping into the woods. In spring, a variety of wildflowers will be blooming. Inside, help yourself to a cup of tea and deposit a dollar recommended donation. Follow the trail to one of their camps in the camas meadows.

Nature trail at Lolo Pass in May!

☙ **Powell Ranger Station**, 13m W of Lolo Pass on Hwy. 12, 208-942-3113, visitor services have been moved to Lolo Pass.

Corp camped here on Sept 14, 1805 and killed one of their colts for food.

☙ **Powell Junction**, from Lochsa Lodge on Hwy. 12, head N on FR 569 (rough road)

Near here the men spent their last night in Idaho in 1806 and finally left Idaho after a long sojourn through the snow of the bitterroots. Without the help of the Nez Perce, it is probable the men would not have been successful in crossing.

☙ **Colt Killed Creek**, exit Hwy. 12 at Lochsa Lodge/Powell Ranger Station, take FS road 102 for 2.2m to the confluence of Colt Killed Creek and the Crooked Fork.

The creek was named by Lewis and Clark in September 1805 because here they butchered a colt to eat.

- **Lochsa Historical Ranger Station**, MM 121.5 Hwy 12, 208-926-4274, 9-5pm summer, visitor center is in the Alternate Ranger's cabin, map and brochure

  The station shows visitors what a ranger station looked like in the 1920's. The station was used from 1925-1950's as a backcountry ranger station and in 1976 was made an interpretive site on the National Register of Historic Places. Use the brochure and take the short walking tour.

> Take a break at the **Lochsa Lodge** (115 Powell Rd, 208-942-3405, http://www.lochsalodge.com/index.php/lochsa/lochsa_lodge) for a meal and/or lodging. The lodge backs up to the Lochsa river with picnic tables on the lawn overlooking the river. Cabins and lodge rooms are rustic with quilts on the beds and pine log walls and ceilings with some wood stoves and separate sitting areas all nestled within the woods. Sandwiches and soup for lunch and steaks, chicken and pasta for dinner. Don't miss huckleberry pancakes.

- **Howard Creek**, 18.5m W of Lolo on Hwy. 12, picnic area, vault toilet, 6am-10pm, .4m difficult loop includes part of the Lewis and Clark trail. Interpretive signs of the expedition.

- **Lolo Hot Springs**, 38500 W. Hwy. 12, 877-541-5117, http://www.lolohotsprings.com/.

  The corps camped here after taking baths in the springs on Sept 13, 1805 and June 29, 1806. Now the springs are commercially operated and include bar, restaurant, casino, pools and lodging. Snowmobiling trails.

- **Lolo Trail/ Lolo Motorway**, FR 500, brochure, no services, from Lolo MT to Weippe Prairie ID. The closest access is at the Lolo Pass Visitor Center.

  The historic Lolo Trail has been used for centuries to cross the Bitterroot Mountains. Today, the trail roughly parallels Hwy. 12. The Motorway is FR 500, largely primitive route even today. It's a good idea to take the brochure with you on the route as well as a 4-wheel drive vehicle.

  The original Lolo trail was used by Native peoples and then Lewis and Clark in Sept. 1805 (taking ten arduous days) and 1806 (a quicker 5 day trip). They left traveler's rest on Sept 11, 1805 and headed west crossing the bitterroot divide. The expedition sought out horses to help them cross. They also received help from Old Toby, a Shoshone guide. This was one of the roughest and most unknown passages on the trip where the group had to cut their own road and the horses constantly slipped down the cliff sides.

They crossed the trail on Sept 11, 1805, taking 10 days to go 150 miles coming out near Weippe. They headed west to the Clearwater River and to Orofino. They returned in 1806 on a similar route running into trouble in early May because of the snow and had to wait for several weeks before the pass was open.

Wendover Ridge, Hwy. 12 to FR 5621 N. 7m hiking trail follows the Lewis and Clark Lolo Trail route.

After staying along the banks of the Lochsa River in Sept 1805, Lewis and Clark realize that they have to climb the canyon to the ridgelines above. It's a 2m switchback climb to the ridgeline and then 6m along the ridge for 3000 feet of climbing. Interpretive signs on the trail.

Lewis wrote:
"... the pleasure I now felt in having tryumphed over the rockey Mountains and decending once more to a level and fertile country where there was every rational hope of finding a comfortable subsistence for myself and party can be more readily conceived than expressed, nor was the flattering prospect of the final success of the expedition less pleasing ..."

Fort Fizzle Historic Site, 4.5m W of Lolo on US12, picnic area, interpretive panels, fishing, restrooms.

Lewis and Clark passed through this area on the Lolo Trail, but the fort was built to stop the advance of Chief Joseph in the Nez Perce wars in 1877.

Orofino Idaho

At the intersection of US 12 and ID7.

The men constructed canoes near here on the banks of the Clearwater River in October 1805. And on May 9th, 1806, the Nez Perce returned 21 of the corps horses to them after caring for the horses for the winter.

Take a break at **Augie's Deli** (202 Johnson Ave, 208-476-5450), a quaint and friendly place for a banana split, a cup of coffee or a sandwich. A few outside tables for people watching.

Clearwater Historical Museum, 315 College Ave, 208-476-5033, http://www.clearwatermuseum.org/, 12:30-4:30, call for hours

Exhibits include artifacts from the Nez Perce and the Lewis and Clark expedition. Clark came through the area in Sept 1805 seeking wood for canoes. Nearby, they spent two weeks making 5 canoes.

- **Dworshank Dam and Fish Hatchery**, 276 Dworshak Complex Dr, cross the river at Orofino to the East side and follow old Hwy. 7 (Riverside/Ahsahka Rd) NW to the dam, 208-476-1255, 9-3pm.

  Small Lewis and Clark display and movie upon request.

- **Canoe Camp**, 14224 US 12, 4m W of Orofino, adjacent to the Clearwater River, 208-843-7009, restrooms, interpretive sign.

  Here Lewis and Clark worked with the Nez Perce from Sept 26-Oct 7 1805 to carve the canoes they needed to get to the Pacific. By the time the corps met up with the Nez Perce they were starving after their struggles to get through the Lolo pass. The Nez Perce diet was heavy in salmon and Camas root both foods that were unfamiliar to the corps, making them very sick. The men managed, however, to carve out 5 canoes in the 12 days they were here.

Kamiah

S of Orofino on US 12.

Kamiah was the winter home of the Nez Perce for centuries. Lewis and Clark were their first white contacts.

Clark wrote of the Nez Perce

"These people has shewn much greater acts of hospitality then we have witnessed from any nation or tribe since we have passed the rocky mountains."

- **Camp Chopunnish (Long Camp) near Kamiah**, MM 68 on Hwy. 12, 1.3m E from Kamiah, interpretive panel. The actual camp is on private land.

  After the men attempted to cross the Bitterroots and discovered the snow blocked their way, they settled down with the Nez Perce in "Long Camp" for three weeks in Spring 1806 from May 14-June 10. The camp was 1/2m downriver of the grain elevators at Kamiah on the Clearwater River.

  Here, Lewis collected a variety of plants and noted his encounters with bears, birds and toads. About ¼ of the plant specimens that Lewis notes came from this area. Sergeant Ordway and a few men were sent out to find Salmon at the Snake River. While they were successful in finally locating salmon (along Hells Canyon), the catch was rotting by the time they returned. They were finally able to depart on June 10th.

  Lewis wrote on May 17th, *"I am pleased at finding the river rise so rapidly, it now doubt is attributeable to the melting snows of the mountains; that icy barier which seperates me from my friends and country, from all which makes life esteemable. - patience, patience."*

  Jefferson's goal of promoting and encouraging relations with the Native Tribes was highly successful for Lewis and Clark in relation to the Nez Perce who served to be true friends, unlike the Native Peoples at the Dalles. Unfortunately, America's record with the Nez Perce after the expedition was largely destructive and self-serving.

Take a break at the **Hearthstone Lodge** (Hwy. 12, MP 64, 208-935-1492) for a few nights lodging and for breakfast and baked goods in their bakery. Great decks for outdoor views and plush decorated rooms in a contemporary lodge.

Weippe

From Kamiah, N on US12 to ID 11 W.

The town is located near the Nez Perce camp where Lewis and Clark reunited after crossing the Bitterroots.

- **Weippe Prairie**, Sw on N Main St to Hwy. 11 S. Where 11 makes a hard left, continue straight on E. Pierce St. to Cemetery Rd. Turn right and head east to Larson Road and turn left. Head south several hundred years and you will see the pullout About 3m S of the town is the approximate spot Clark entered the prairie. Interpretive Sign.

  274 acres of the over 3000-acre prairie is accessible to the public as the Nez Perce National Historical Park. The blue Camas flowers bloom between May and June and while close-up you are unlikely to mistake the meadow for a lake, the sea of blue is pretty amazing.

  In September 1805, the Corps descended the Lolo Trail into the Weippe prairie which spanned over three thousand acres and was a welcome change from the rugged Rockies. Here they also met up with friendly Nez Perce. They stayed with the group led by "Chief Twisted Hair" for two and half weeks learning about the flora, fauna and the chance of a water route to the Pacific. The Nez Perce had chosen this area for their home because of the abundance of the Camas Plant that grew in the prairie, a prime source of food. In mid-October, the Corps set out from the Nez Perce in their canoes on Clearwater River, hoping it would take them to the Pacific. On their return trip, the corps also stayed with the Nez Perce for over a month as they waited for snow to melt. The corps ate so many Camus tubers, and it was such an abrupt change in their meat heavy diet, that they got very sick.

- **Weippe Discovery Center**, Wood St, 208-435-4406, http://www.weippediscoverycenter.com/, 10-5, closed Sun, 10-1 on Sat.

  This new interpretive center includes exterior murals of the Lewis and Clark landscape. Take a walk around the center and read the quotes from the journals. Travel the outside interpretive trail that focuses on the mountain and prairie plants identified by Lewis and Clark (these are some of the better plaques on the plants identified by the expedition). A good selection of replica tools that Lewis and Clark used are on display. The public library here also has a good selection of Lewis and Clark books. Note that the murals and trail can be viewed when the center is closed. While small, this center is worth a stop if you are in the area.

Cottonwood

From Kamiah, Cottonwood is S on ID 162 about 28 miles.

* **Historical Museum at St Gertrude**, 465 Keuterville Rd, Cottonwood ID, 208-962-7123, https://www.historicalmuseumatstgertrude.org/, 9-4:30, closed Dun, $6 adult, $3 student.

  Eclectic museum focuses on the regional history with a splash of European and Asian artifacts from the 14th century.

Take a break at the **Inn at St Gertrude**, 208-451-4321, https://www.innatstgertrude.com/, run by the Benedictine Sisters of Idaho. Four rooms or suites are simply but comfortably furnished and include air condition and private baths. The inn is on the Monastery grounds and invites exploration of the surrounding forest. It's a peaceful place with full amenities.

Lapwai/Spalding

NE from Cottonwood, Lapwai is 45 miles on US 95.

* **Nez Perce National Historical Park/Spalding Visitor Center**, 39063 Hwy. 95, 3m N of Lapwai, 208-843-7001, 8-5pm summer, closes at 4:30 rest of the year, grounds are open sunrise to sunset, movie, museum, trails, Map, River Trail Guide,

  The focus is on the history of the Nez Perce but included is the Lewis and Clark Peace Medal.

* **The Northwest Discovery Water Trail**, 40m reach of the Clearwater River from Canoe Camp to the confluence of the Snake in Lewiston Idaho (trail continues into the Columbia River Gorge), http://www.ndwt.org/ndwt/index.asp . 150 spots to launch a boat, picnic, camp.

Winchester

Off US95 W on Bus 95

* **Museum of Winchester History**, 417 McBeth Ave, 208-924-7920

  Exhibit on Sergeant Ordway's search for the salmon needed to feed the expedition.

Lewiston/Clarkston

Lewiston and Clarkston are named after Lewis and Clark and sit next to one another across the Snake River. Lewiston is on the Idaho side, Clarkston on the Washington side. US95 comes in from Idaho and heads N out of Lewiston. US 12 runs through both Lewiston and Clarkson's N edge.

One of the many disappointments for today's travelers is how much of the natural landscape has altered from Lewis and Clark's vivid descriptions in the journals. The 300-mile route between Lewiston and the Bonneville Dam is particularly changed as the result of eight dams on the Snake and Columbia. The Snake River dams are under consideration today for removal to improve the Salmon runs. It's possible that we may soon see some of the rock formations and rapids that Lewis and Clark described that are currently drowned.

- **Highway US12W to WA14W**, The highway between Clarkston and Ilwaco has been designated the Lewis and Clark Trail highway. Interpretive signs are erected throughout this route. Map.

- **Snake and Clearwater Confluence Center**, 502 Bridge St, parking lot at the West end of D st., 509-758-7712

  Along a walking path on the levee near the confluence of the Clearwater and Snake rivers sits a historical marker for Oct 10, 1805 and interpretive displays. From the levee, visitors can see the Snake and Clearwater Rivers, Hells Canyon, and on a clear day, all the way to the Bitterroot Mountains. A dug out canoe is visible as well.

- **Chief Timothy Park and Confluence Project**, 13766 US 12, 8m W of Clarkston, 509-758-9580, open 24-hours, camping, flush toilets, hiking trails, swimming, playground

  Interpretive artwork by Maya Lin to reflect the people of the Columbia River Basin. In this installation visitors can enjoy the artwork in an environment that very much still resembles how Lewis and Clark would have experience it with native grasses and, in spring, wildflowers.

🏛 **Nez Perce County Historical Museum**, 306 Third St, 208-743-2535, Tues-Sat 10-4, $4 adults, $2 students.

Lewis and Clark exhibits focus on the Nez Perce interactions with Lewis and Clark.

Dig a Little Deeper

The Nez Perce (Nimiipu) inhabited the area from North Dakota to Oregon that Lewis and Clark traveled through. In this 27 minute video, learn about the Nez Perce culture and history from the Nez Perce. When Lewis and Clark met the Nez Perce, they were thriving economically because of their location within the middle of trade routes. They were well known to the other tribes and highly respected. Lewis and Clark benefited from their interaction with the Nez Perce, but the Nez Perce were also dramatically affected by their arrival and the subsequent wave of White Europeans that flooded their land. In 1805, there were at least 8000 Nez Perce. By 1899 there were less than 1600. The video states that both Clark and York had children with Nez Perce women. The video focuses on how the Nez Perce helped the corps and then on the influence the corps had convincing the Nez Perce to want to acquire some of the white people's benefits including medicine and religion. Eventually, the video also shows the negative effects of the whites including disease and resettlement. The video includes a brief history of the Lewis and Clark expedition as well as maps but the focus is on the interaction between the two peoples. On Feb 15, 1806, Lewis described the Nez Perce horses, one of their greatest treasures.

🏛 **Lewis and Clark State College Center for Art and History**, 415 Main St, 5th and Main, 208-792-2243, http://www.lcsc.edu/cah/, 11-4, closed Sun.

Tools of the expedition and Seaman displays. Changing exhibits. Check website.

Take a break in Lewiston at **Waffles N' More** (1421 Main St, 208-743-5189) for hearty breakfasts and Belgian waffles with piles of whipped cream, or the **Mystic Café** (1303 Main St, 208-743-1811, http://themysticcafe.com/) for locally sourced, high quality breakfast, lunches or dinners. This is one of our favorites. Love the Gyro Bowl and the lamb burger. Head to Clarkston for pizza, pasta and steak at **Tomato Bros** (200 Bridge St, 509-758-7902, http://tomatobrothers.com/) or just about anything. Huge menu.

🏛 **Granite Lake Park**, 850 Port Way, Clarkson, picnic areas, restrooms, walking path.

This is a good place to see some of the native plants that Lewis wrote about. Good views of the Snake river.

🏛 **Pioneer Park,** 203 5th St, 5th St, 3 blocks S of Main, 208-746-2313.

Bronze Sacagawea fountain by Shirley Bothum surrounded by four coyotes created by Sharon Taylor.

🏛 **Hells Gate State Park Lewis and Clark Discovery Center**, 4832 Hells Gate State Rd, 4m S of Lewiston, 208-799-5015, camping, picnic tables, laundry, showers, hiking and mountain biking trails, swimming beach. Park entrance fee.

The Discovery Center is located four miles from the original Lewis and Clark route to the Pacific and includes a very thorough view of the expedition. Indoor educational displays and an outdoor interpretive plaza with a teepee, canoe and raptor exhibit. Interpretive displays include a large topographical map, canoe and panels on meeting of two cultures, how the expedition ate, their "healthcare", and Ordway's Salmon trip nearby in May 1806. One of the few places with a display on Weetxuwiis, the young Nez Perce woman who spoke up for Lewis and Clark when the Nez Perce contemplated killing the group. And, some of the panels are from the perspective of Nez Perce oral history. Movie "From the Mountains to the Sea: Lewis & Clark in Idaho". Center overlooks the Snake River. Be sure to check out the moving stream with sculptures by Rip Caswell that extends out into the Snake River. Access to Levee Path for walking and/or biking. This is a good place to get a different perspective on the expedition and to visit for a few hours, especially with children. Lots of room outside to run around.

🏛 **Confluence Overlook**, 8m N of Lewiston on Hwy. 95, turn left onto Spur Rd followed by a quick right turn onto Beacon Dr and then right onto Old Spiral Hwy and then another quick right onto Hwy 95S for 1.4m to pullout. (this is different from the overlook in town).

🏛 **Lewis and Clark Enter Washington Interpretive Sign**, 1 1/2m W of Clarkston on US12, map and brief discussion of the corps entrance into Washington.

🏛 **Lewis and Clark Alpowa Summit**, 20m W of Clarkston on US12, brief introductory sign on the corps in Washington.

Washington/Oregon

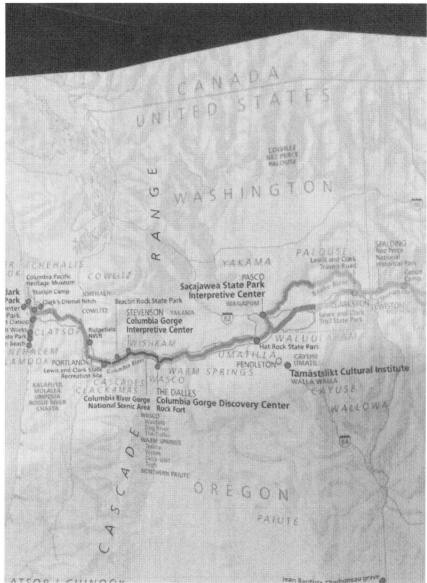

Washington and Oregon, along the Columbia river, are an area of contrasts. The Eastern side of the states are dry, desert-like and continues as such until The Dalles. As you head west from The Dalles, the rainfall increases one inch for each mile. You don't have to go far along the river before you will notice an increase in forests, green shrubs and rain. The

Columbia River Basalt Group (CRBG) is the dominant rock formation that Lewis and Clark would have viewed as they traveled down the Columbia River. On the Eastern side, the CRBG will often be easily visible but on the western part it is often overgrown with trees.

The CRBG was the result of basalt eruptions during the Miocene Epoch, 16-15.6 million years ago. It was one of the largest basaltic lava flows ever. And for 10-15 million years, lava periodically poured out eventually accumulating to over 6000 ft.

The Columbia River Gorge was not created by the Great Lake Missoula floods but instead was the result of CRBG flood basalt deposition, anticline and syncline folding as the area experienced intense compression stress. Three million years ago, the Cascades began their monumental rise over 3000 ft which resulted in the deepening entrenchment of the Columbia River carving away at the CRBG. The gorge was the result.

Lewis and Clark entered Washington on Oct 10, 1805 hoping for signs of the Pacific. They had no idea how big the area was they would have to navigate before they finally located it. For some reason, Lewis also stopped keeping his journal from Sept. 1 to Jan 1, so the records of this part of the expedition are limited. And, in contrast to the struggles over the bitterroot, travel up the Clearwater, Snake and Columbia moved much more quickly leaving less time for journaling.

General

Washington State Park Discover Pass, $30 allows entry to state parks and recreation areas. One pass can be shared among two vehicles. Purchase online.

Northwest Forest Pass, day pass is $5, $30 for an annual pass for both Oregon and Washington. Passes required at several of the Lewis and Clark spots: Bridge of the Gods, North Bonneville. Forest pass.

Oregon State Parks Pass, 21 Oregon State Parks in the gorge area require a pass. Day pass is $5, annual pass is $30.

Almota

S of Colfax at the end of WA 194 on the banks of the Snake River. The Corps camped at the mouth of Almota Creek on Oct. 11, 1805.

🏚 **Boyer Park**, 1753 Granite Rd, WA 195 to Lower Granite Rd E along the Snake, 509-397-3208, full service marina, camping, cabins, restrooms, store, picnic tables, 4.5m snake river trail, interpretive sign.

Lewis and Clark stopped here, camping Oct 11, 1805, and bought fish and dogs from the Nez Perce.

Pomeroy

US 12, 23m W of Lewiston and Clarkston

🏚 **Lewis and Clark Travois Road**, crosses Hwy 12 at Pataha Creek, 5m East of Pomeroy.

These are some of the last surviving evidence of the travois marks, made by two poles attached to a dog or horse, because most of the surrounding area has been farmed. Lewis and Clark did not make the Travois marks, but they used the trail on May 3rd, 1806. It was once used extensively by the Nez Perce, Walla Walla and Cayuse and later by fur trappers and settlers.

Dayton

US 12 travels through Dayton, 24m from Pomeroy. The Touchet River runs through town as well.

🏛 **Lewis and Clark Trail State Park**, 36149 Hwy. 12, 6m W of Dayton, 509-337-6457, discover pass, picnic tables, camping, fishing, hiking, birding, restrooms, showers, Map.

37-acre state park with almost 1400 ft of freshwater shoreline on the Touchet River. Interpretive displays on Lewis and Clark, who camped here May 2, 1806, and homesteaders in the area. The park spans both sides of Hwy. 12. On the S side is a birding trail and picnic tables. On the north side is river access, a hiking trail and camping.

Take a break at the **Weinhard Hotel and Café** (235 E Main St, 509-382-4032, https://www.weinhard.com/) for a Victorian experience. Rooms are decorated with a mix of Victorian antiques and modern conveniences. There is an espresso bar and a rooftop garden which make this a good choice for a couple day layover. The café (509-382-1681), across the street, serves soup, salad and sandwiches.

★ **Historic Depot and Boldman House**, 222 E Commercial St, 509-382-2026, http://www.daytonhistoricdepot.org/, Depot is open 10-5 Weds-Sat

History of the area.

🏛 **Patit Creek Campsite**, 2m E of Dayton on Patit Rd, 509-337-6457, camping

This is an unusual site with Silhouette statues representing the corps at the turn off. There is a statue for each participant. The corps passed through Dayton on their return journey on May 2nd, 1806. While there is not much interpretive material available at the site, it's kind of interesting to see.

🏛 **Palus Artifact and Homestead Museum**, 426 E Main St, 509-540-9560, April-Nov 1-4 Fri and Sat.

Artifacts from the Palouse Indian tribe and exhibits on the Lewis and Clark expedition.

Perry/Joso

WA 261 at the Snake River

🏕 **Lyons Ferry State Park**, On MT 261, US 12 N of Dayton, turn W on MT 261, restrooms, picnic tables, swimming, fishing. Discover pass.

Lyons ferry is at the intersection of the Snake River and the Palouse. Drewyers River Heritage Marker. At the Palouse, in Oct 1805 the corps found great fishing and evidence that this area was regularly used by the Native Americans as a fishing area. The area is also of geological significance. It is the dividing point for the Ice Age floods more than 13, 000 years ago.

Ayer
Lyons Ferry Rd SW to Ayer Rd

🏕 **Ayer at the Snake**, Ayer Rd W from Lyons Ferry Rd, S of Lyons Ferry State Park

Oct 13, the corps camped here on the S side of the Snake along with a couple of Native Americans. Clark noted that Sacagawea was instrumental in befriending the different Indians.

Walla Walla
US 12 and WA 125 intersect in Walla Walla near the Oregon border.

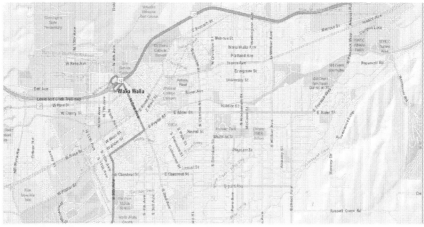

The Walla Walla Indians and their chief Yelleppit met up with the expedition in Oct, 1805 as the corps pushed west. The corps had declined to stop on their way to the Pacific because they were in such a hurry but promised to return. They re-entered the area in April 1806 and visited Yelleppit's village of 15 lodges where they were warmly welcomed. The corps was quite lucky because a captured Shoshone translated Walla Walla into Shoshone for Sacagawea who translated for the corps thus enabling communication.

✦ **Whitman Mission NHS**, 328 Whitman Mission Rd, Walla Walla, 509-522-6360, https://www.nps.gov/whmi/index.htm, visitor center, self-guided trail, picnic areas, restrooms.

The Whitmans came to Washington to convert the Native Americans. Instead, they were killed whether for revenge or retribution is still largely unknown. But the Natives faced widespread disease after the missionaries arrival and immigrants were coming in by the hundreds. The Cayuse attacked the mission in 1847, killing 14 people. This site explores the complex intersection of the Missionaries and the Native Peoples.

- **Fort Walla Walla Museum**, 755 Myra Rd, 509-525-7703, http://www.fwwm.org/#world-wars, 10-5, $8 adults, $3 children.

  17 building pioneer settlement, gardens, exhibit halls make this a place for a day long visit. A Lewis and Clark exhibit focuses on their journey in this region. Life-size diorama of Clark meeting Yellept of the Walla Wallas

> Take a break in one of many, many Walla Walla restaurants. There is a little of everything here. But **Graze** (5 S Colville St, 509-522-9991) is an excellent stop for visitors for healthy salads and sandwiches or even a to-go lunch.

Wallula

On US 12 at Lake Wallula, E of the Tri-Cities. Wallula sits a bit north of the Confluence of the Columbia and the Walla Walla Rivers. Campsite for Oct 18, 1805 was nearby but is now under water.

History of Wallula

> Take a break: one of the nicest places to stay and a bit unexpected in this area is the **Cameo Heights Mansion** in Touchet (1072 Oasis Rd, 509-394-0211, https://cameoheightsmansion.com/blog/2017/03/lewis-and-clark-trail-state-park/).

Wallula Junction

S of Wallula where Hwy. 12 and 730 intersect and where the Walla Walla comes into the Columbia.

- **Wallula Gap**, on WA 730 at MP 4.8 along the river, http://ww2020.net/historic-sites/wallula/. Fishing, hiking trails, Interpretive signage, brochure.

  Details the important history of the area. Great views overlooking the Columbia river and you can clearly see the "gap". On April 27, 1806, Lewis and Clark met up with Yelleppit for the second time, and they spend several days with him near the confluence of the Walla Walla and the Columbia Rivers. Yelleppit was very helpful in drawing a map of the Snake and Columbia river confluence, and Lewis gave him one of the peace medals. This area is largely accessible through the McNary National Wildlife Refuge.

Burbank

US 12 and WA 124, across the river from Pasco WA.

After a few mishaps and canoes capsizing, the Corps reached the confluence of the Snake and Columbia on Oct 16, 1805. They set up camp at the site of Sacajawea State Park in what is now Pasco (see below).

🏛 **Ice Harbor Dam Visitor Center**, 2339 Monument Dr, off MT 124, 5.5m E of Burbank WA, 509-547-2048, 9-4:30 April-Oct, restrooms.

Several movies are available, one is "Lewis and Clark: Confluence of Time and Courage", which focuses on their full trip (60 minutes). Interactive displays and programs.

✦ **McNary National Wildlife Refuge**, 64 Maple St, US 12 SE from Pasco, 509-546-8300, sunrise-sunset, 8-4 for headquarters Mon-Fri. trails, wildlife viewing, education center.

Spans the east bank of the Columbia from the Snake to the Wallula gap. Many of the birds at the refuge were the same Clark recorded in his journal. 1m trail around the lake is a great opportunity for bird watching.

Tri-City Area

While each of the cities in the Tri-City area are discussed separately below, there are a few useful tips for navigating this area.

Kennewick is on the S side of the Columbia, W of Richland. Pasco is on the N side of the Columbia and Richland is on the S side of the Columbia.

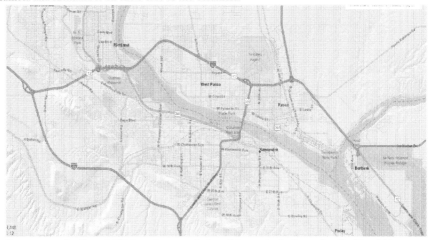

Freeway navigation: I 182 is a freeway designed to navigate from the N side of Pasco through Richland and connect to I82 which runs along the S side of Kennewick and

Richland. US 395 Connects the I82 at Kennewick's S side to Pasco and I82 making a circle. WA 240 runs through the center of this circle along the S side of the Columbia River.

Trails: The Columbia Park Trail runs from Richland, just to the SW side of I82 where the Walmart SuperCenter sits (off Queensgate Dr. S) to the Ed Hendler Bridge at the Columbia River that crosses from Kennewick into Pasco. Windmill Rd, off the Columbia Park Trail, connects to a bike/walking path that goes both N and to the Yakima. The trail runs similarly on the other side of the river from the Ed Hendler Bridge to Chiawana Park in West Pasco (you can bike and/or walk across the I182 bridge). Map and Information. The Sacajawea Heritage trail listed below is a part of this larger trail.

Richland

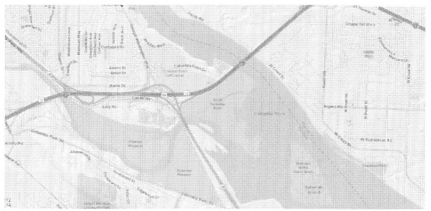

🚲 **Sacajawea Heritage Trail**, Access at Columbia Point Marina at I-182/US 12, 23m paved blacktop trail along the Columbia River that connects Pasco, Richland and Kennewick, with a focus on both education and recreation, picnic areas, camping at nearby Hood Park, Map

Interpretive panels along the way on natural and historical topics. Trail connects at Columbia Point Marina to the Richland Riverfront Trail. Much of the trail is scenic as it passes through parks and nature areas, but sections, like that near Pasco, can be quite industrial. The bridge crossings are on separated trails from the traffic, but the crossings can be noisy and the trail narrow. If you want the most scenic part of the trail and least traffic, stick to the Richland to Kennewick section of the trail starting from Columbia Park and traveling on the East side of Hwy. 240. After passing the Riverview nature preserve, turn left and stay along the riverside trail and then ride into Bateman Island. The corps traveled to Bateman on Oct 17, 1805, the furthest up the Columbia River the corps journeyed. The ride that continues along Columbia Park is also pleasant and takes you to the Reach Interpretive Center, see below.

Take a break and have a beer. While Washington is known for its wine, beer has also taken off and in the Tri-cities you have many choices. **Ice Harbor Brewery** (206 N Benton St, Kennewick, 509-582-5340, http://iceharbor.com/) with typical pub fare; **Barley's Brewpub** (3320 W. Kennewick Ave, Kennewick), 509-221-1534, http://www.barleysbrewhub.com/), 40 tap handles including wine and cider and bbq sandwiches; **Bombing Range Brewing** (2000 Logston Blvd, Richland, 509-392-3377, http://bombingrangebrewing.com/) focuses on lagers and ales and serves pizza; **White Bluffs Brewing** (2034 Logston Blvd, Richland, 509-578-4558) usually has a food truck on site and an outside patio; **Shrub Steppe Smokehouse Brewery** (701 The Pkwy, Richland, 509-375-9092, http://www.shrubsteppesmokehousebrewery.com/) includes a few guest taps, bbq but get the chili or better yet, the chili dog; **Paper Street Brewing** (701 The Pkwy, 509-713-7088, http://www.paperstreetbrewing.com/); **The Growler Guys** (110 Gage Blvd, 509-491-3600); **Copper Top Tap House** (5453 Ridgeline Dr, Ste 110, Kennewick, 509-572-9067, http://www.coppertoptaphouse.com/index.html) bring your own food. Order a tasting sampler. Most have food or allow you to bring food in from outside.

- ✦ **Chamna Natural Preserve**, S Richland on the Yakima River between the two major Interstate interchanges, from I182 E, take exit 4 and take the first right to Aaron Drive. From I182 W take exit 5B and then the first left onto Aaron Dr. Head to Jadwin Ave to go over I182 to Carrier Rd N (getting here can be confusing), 509-942-7529, 11m trail access, birding, access to water trails including the Tapteal Water trail. Interpretive signs identify the flora and fauna. Information.

- ✦ **The Reach Interpretive Center**, 1943 Columbia Park Trail, Richland, 509-943-4100, http://www.visitthereach.org/, can be reached along the Sacajawea Heritage Trail at N. Columbia Center Blvd. $10 adult, $6 students, 10-4:30, closed Sun-Mon.

  The main focus is the Hanford Reach Reactor but exhibits also include geology. Outside views over the Columbia River. If you are interested in Hanford, this is a highly recommended stop. It also has one of the best geology exhibits for understanding the area geology.

- 🏛 **Lewis & Clark Interpretive Overlook**, Columbia Center Blvd and Columbia Park Trail, interpretive panels and map.

  Views of the Columbia River

- 🏛 **Columbia River Journeys**, 509-734-9941, https://www.columbiariverjourneys.com/custom-tours/

  Group interpretive tours of Lewis and Clark expedition.

> Take a break at **Porter's Real BBQ** (705 The Pkwy, 509-942-9590), simple hearty slow smoked BBQ made in-house. Hard to recommend anything specific. It's all good.

Pasco

- **Franklin County Historical Museum**, 305 N 4th Ave, 509-547-3714, https://franklincountyhistoricalsociety.org/, 12-5 Wed-Fri, 9:30-2:30 Sat-Sun.

  Local history. Exhibits on Native Americans, pioneers and aviation in a 1910 Carnegie Library building.

- **Sacajawea State Park & Interpretive Center**, 2503 Sacajawea Park Rd, Pasco, 509-542-2361, 8am-dusk summer, closed Nov 1-Mar 31, restrooms, picnic facilities, 1.2m trail, boat dock. Discover Pass. Map.

  The Corps arrived at the confluence of the Snake and Columbia on Oct 16, 1805 where they camped for two nights. Here they met with a large number of the Yakima and the Wanapams who welcomed them with drums and dancing. The corps purchased dogs for dinner. They also first wrote about cradle boards after this stop. They stayed here for two nights.

  Focus is on Sacajawea and the Lewis and Clark journey as well as Native American History. Lewis and Clark camped nearby on Oct 16 and 17, 1805. The Interpretive center includes interactive exhibits on the Corps, Sacajawea and the tribes of the region. Of especial interest are the seven story circle installations in the 267-acre park created by artist Maya Lin. Take the interpretive walk to read about Native peoples.

  Access to the Sacagawea Heritage Trail is 1/4m before entering the state park.

- **Snake River Confluence**, 2503 Sacajawea Park Rd,

  On Oct 16, 1805 Lewis and Clark reached this confluence of the Snake and Columbia.

- **Sacajawea Roadside Interpretive Marker**, Hwy. 12 and Sacajawea Park Rd. Interpretive sign on Sacajawea and how she aided the expedition.

- **Lewis & Clark Commemorative Marker**, Entrance to Hood Park on the Snake River at the Hwy 12 and 124 intersection.

Kennewick

Take a break at **Masala Indian Cuisine** (3321 N Kennewick Ave Ste 100, 509-737-9999) and enjoy some mildly spicy Punjabi cuisine in a colorful dining room. Get the dosa and the lamb vindaloo.

- **East Benton County Historical Museum**, 205 Keewaydin Dr, 509-582-7704, http://www.ebchs.org/, Tues–Sat 12–4. $5 adults, $1 youth.

    Good exhibit of Kennewick man, Native Americans and explorers and pioneers.

Oregon

Many of the Columbia Gorge Trails cross an area or walk a path that Lewis and Clark toured (and many are listed below), but for general hiking, this is a great site. Note however that the Eagle Creek Fire in 2017 closed many trails or parts of trails. So check the website for updates. Columbia Gorge Hiking Trails

Multiple paths are available for bikers through the Gorge area, Columbia River Gorge Bike Map

Affordable and convenient bus service throughout the Gorge area. Also provide service from open parking lots to waterfalls where the lots are full or closed. Columbia Gorge Express

Map of many of the Lewis and Clark sties along the Columbia River

Oregon State Park Pass

Pendleton

S of the Tri-Cities on I 84.

- **Tamasksilikit Cultural Institute**, 47106 Wildhorse Blvd, Pendleton, exit 216 on I 84, 541-966-9748, http://www.tamastslikt.org/, 10–5, closed Sun, $10 adult, $6 youth, café. Interpretive center on the Umatilla Indian reservation. Exhibits on some of the Indians that the Corps encountered.

- **Pendleton River Parkway**, Westgate Pl and Umatilla River between SE Byers Ave and SE Court Pl, 2.5m trail. Park at 1205 SW Court Ave at Roy Raley Park or 413 SE Byers at Stillman Park, restrooms.

Take a Break at the **Great Pacific Wine and Coffee Co**. (403 S Main St, 541-276-1350, http://greatpacific.biz/) for a glass of wine or a cup of coffee for sure, but also for a pizza or sandwich. And, if they have them, get a raspberry croissant.

Umatilla

I82 runs through Umatilla N to S. Umatilla is a rural desert community where the Umatilla river enters the Columbia. Lots of parks and beachfront. The Two Rivers Correctional Institution is located here.

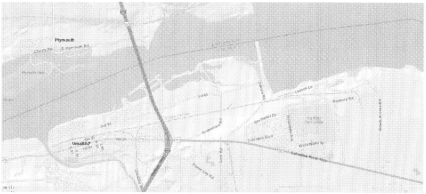

Umatilla is the Indian word for "water rippling over sand".

- 🏛 **Lewis and Clark Expedition interpretive marker,** Devore Rd N of 6ᵗʰ St, on the west side of the road. Several panels provide a map and brief explanation of the corps and panels on local Lewis and Clark events. It's worth a stop here when you arrive.

- 🏛 **McNary Wildlife Nature Area Lock and Dam,** 82790 Devore Rd, 509-546-8300, dawn to dusk, restrooms interpretive signs describe the rapids, Pacific Salmon Visitor Information Center (541-922-3211, 9am-4pm), picnic tables, hiking, fishing

   The trailhead for the Lewis and Clark trail is located at the east end of the park.

- 🏛 **Umatilla County Lewis & Clark Commemorative Trail,** Warehouse Beach Recreation Area, 9.5m E of Umatilla on Hwy. 730, exit right at Hwy. 37, also accessible at Hat Rock and the McNary Wildlife Nature Area. trailhead, picnic tables, restrooms, 7.3m trail crosses the cliffs along the Columbia River with some steep, sandy sections. Very little shade.

- ✦ **Spillway Park,** Devore Rd past the McNary Dam main parking, 541-922-2268, restrooms, picnic tables, overlooks from which to view the McNary Dam.

- 🏛 **LePage Park,** 5m from Rufus, 541-739-1135, confluence of John Day and Columbia Rivers, interpretive signs, camping, fishing, swimming, restrooms

   The park is named after Private Jean Baptiste LePage.

✦ **Umatilla National Wildlife Refuge**, 10m S of I84 at the end of Paterson Ferry Rd, sunrise to sunset, restrooms, hunting, auto tour, fishing, hiking

Hermiston
S of Umatilla on US 395.

🏛 **Hat Rock State Park**, east of Umatilla Oregon off US 730, 541-983-2277, hiking, picnic tables, restrooms, interpretive signs, fishing, swimming, boating. Brochure

The 70ft high rock was first distinctive landmark that Lewis and Clark passed on the Columbia that has not been submerged by dams. Hat Rock is a remnant of a 12-million year old basalt flow. It is likely that the rock has long stood as a landmark far before Lewis and Clark arrived. Trees provide needed shade. Interpretive signs tell the story of the expedition. A historic trail runs from Hat Rock to the McNary Beach park following the expedition along the cliffs of the Columbia River. Roundtrip is 10m.

🏛 **Sand Station Recreation Area**, N of Hat Rock on US 730, vault toilets, picnic tables

Located on Lake Wallula's shore, this 8-acre park has great views of the Wallula Gap. Lewis and Clark passed through on Oct 19, 1805 where they viewed many Indian lodges on the other side of the river.

Take a break at **Walker's Farm Kitchen** (920 SE 4th St, 541-289-3333) and enjoy local, farm-fresh lunches and dinners. Pork belly with blueberry habanero or smoked trout salads are excellent.

Irrigon
On the S bank of the Columbia River on US 730.

🏛 **Irrigon Marine Park**, N 7th St, 541-922-4933, boating, picnic areas interpretive signs and hiking trail.

Corps camped just a stone's throw from the park on Oct 19, 1805. They encountered Native People living in lodges made of reed mats. Many of these natives, perhaps Umatilla, weren't accustomed to the "white" people and Clark, with the help of Sacagawea, spent time and gifts calming them. The actual camping area is now under water. Access to Morrow County Columbia River Heritage Trail.

Boardman
I84 runs through Boardman.

* **Sage Center**, 101 Olson Rd, 541-481-7243, http://visitsage.com/home, 10-5, unique visitor center with a focus on agriculture and energy in the area.

* **Boardman Marina Park**, 1 West Marine Dr, 1m off I84, 888-481-7217, restrooms, beach, camping, hiking trails.

* **Columbia River Heritage Trail**, 12m non-motorized recreational trail that goes from Boardman W to Irrigon, http://www.columbiarivertrail.org/. Hiking, biking, bird watching. Trail passes the Lewis and Clark campsite for Oct 19, 1805.

Roosevelt WA

Along WA 14 on the Columbia River.

Lewis and Clark camped near here twice, once on Oct 20, 1805 and again on April 24, 1806.

On WA 14, the corps camped in the Roosevelt vicinity on Oct 20th. Clark noted an Indian burial vault along the route including human skulls and horse skeletons. He speculated that the horses were sacrificed as part of the burial ritual.

Rufus

On US 30 on the Columbia River.

* **John Day Dam**, E on US 30, 541-296-1181

    The Corps spent Oct 21st near the current site of the dam, having traveled 42 miles through many rapids. The nonswimmers portaged while the others navigated the rapids. Today, because of the dams we don't see the rapids.

* **Deschutes River State Recreation Area**, I84 exit 104 SW to Biggs-Rufus Hwy W, 541-739-2322, restrooms, picnic facilities, camping, three trails, fishing, biking.

    The Deschutes runs off the Columbia River,

    Lewis and Clark came upon the Deschutes on Oct 22, 1805, referring to it by its Native American name, "Towarnehiooks". On their return trip on April 21, 1806, when they passed the river, Clark called it "Clarks River".

    Clark wrote,

    "... dureing the time the front of the party was waiting for Cap Lewis, I assended a high hill from which I could plainly See the range of Mountains which runs South from Mt. Hood as far as I could See. ... Clarks river which mouthes imedeately opposit to me forks at about 18 or 20 miles, the West fork runs to the Mt Hood and the main branch Runs from S.E. ..."

Goldendale, WA

US 97 S of I82 exit 50.

🏛 **Maryhill Museum**, 35 Maryhill Museum Dr, S on US97 to WA 14 W, 509-773-3733, http://www.maryhillmuseum.org/, 10-5pm, Mar 15-Nov 15, $12 adults, $5 children, shaded picnic areas, restrooms, nature trail, café.

I really like this museum but don't expect your typical museum. Exhibits are quite eclectic from a variety of outdoor sculptures around the grounds to a chess set collection to a room of Rodin sculptures and another of Native American basketry. It's easy to spend an hour or three here if you visit the indoor and outdoor exhibits and enjoy a lunch on the expansive grounds. The views from everywhere are some of the best you will get on the Columbia. And, the Georgian house is worth a picture or two.

Lewis and Clark enjoyed the views from this area as well. Head to the nature trail along the river at the end of the parking area. Look east to the Sam Hill bridge and you will be enjoying the view Lewis and Clark had of the Columbia river. Many of the plants on the nature trail were identified by Clark.

Take a break at **The Glass Onion** (604 S Columbus Ave, 509-773-4928) for fresh, local food for lunch and dinner and enjoy an eclectic selection including octopus, fish and chips and samosa. It's a good choice. For a more casual breakfast or lunch, try **Bake My Day Bakery and Café** (119 E Main, 509-773-0403). The quiche is usually really good.

🏛 **Maryhill State Park**, 50 US 97, 509-773-5007, April 1-Oct 31, camping, restrooms, 1.1m of trails, fishing, discover pass. Map

Canoe in the Columbia River along the same route as Lewis and Clark from this park. The Corps paddled past the park on Oct. 22, 1805. On the return journey, the corps was mostly on foot and they had to follow the Native trails up and over the high cliffs around the park.

Dallesport, WA

US 197 from the N take Tidyman Rd W and from the S take Dallesport Rd W.

🏛 **Columbia Hills State Park (and Horsethief Lake)**, 85 WA 14, E from US197, 509-767-1159, discover pass, restrooms, picnic tables, interpretive signs, 12 m of hiking trails, camping, rock climbing, swimming, pedal boat rentals, petroglyphs. Guided tours on Fri and Sat at 10am. Call to make a reservation, 509-439-9032. Brochure.

The park offers climbing on Horsethief butte and lots of water sports including paddleboard rentals. A historic homestead is a few miles up the road.

The Corps camped here Oct 22-24 1805 after running "The Narrows" and visiting a nearby Indian village with 20 wooden houses. If the opportunity is made available, go on the guided tour to Tsagaglalal (she who watches). This is rarely viewed because of past vandalism.

On October 24, 1805 Clark wrote, "The natives of this village received me very kindly, one of whom invited me into his house, which I found to be large and commodious, and the first wooden houses in which Indians have lived since we left those in the vicinity of the Illinois; they are 20 feet wide and 30 feet long, with one door raised 18 inches above ground... the roof of them was supported by a ridge pole resting on three strong pieces of split timber, through one of which the door was cut."

The Dalles Area

The Dalles is at the intersection of US 197 and I 84. US 30 runs through the city.

Downtown The Dalles is accessed from the Columbia River. In the downtown area you will find hotels, interesting food trucks (explore the main streets to check out what's available), several brew pubs and coffee shops. Head S from downtown to access the river trail which runs both east and west along the river.

As Lewis and Clark headed West from here, they began their entry into the actual Gorge. And Clark noted the many waterfalls, on the Oregon side, he would encounter that visitors can still enjoy. He wrote on Oct. 29, 1805, *"a butifull cascade falling over a rock of about 100 feet"*. *Clark often referred to these falls as "cascades"*. There are almost no waterfalls noted by Lewis and Clark on the Washington side. This is a result of the geology on the North side of the Columbia. Landslides are common on the Washington side as they slip towards the steep south side of the Gorge. Landslides reduce the angle of the rocks on the Washington side and, thus, also reduce the likelihood of waterfalls on that side.

Their return trip to the Dalles in April 1806 would prove to be one of their most trying with the Native People and the environment. The men struggled to portage their horses and goods through the Dalles. A three day process that was successful if very grueling. To add to their frustration, it was very difficult for Clark to convince the Eneesur village to sell him horses. Lewis wrote that the people in this area were *"poor, dirty, proud, haughty, inhospitable, parsimonious, and faithless in every rispect."* The natives also were regularly steeling and harassing the corps. Lewis was so angry that he threatened to shoot the first Indian he caught attempting to steal from the group. Luckily for all, he did not have to resort to this option, though he did end up punching one thief. One can only imagine their relief when they finally departed the area at the end of April.

> Take a break at one of the many restaurant choices in The Dalles. One good choice is **Petite Provence** (408 E 2nd St, 541-506-0037) which offers a casual, comfortable atmosphere and good breakfasts and lunch. It also offers a wide variety of pastries.

- **Dalles Riverfront Trail**, paved path goes about 10m from Columbia Gorge Discovery Center along the Columbia River to the Dalles Dam. Restrooms at riverfront park. Map.

- **Celilo Park/Falls Portage**, I84, exit 97, view from Celilo Park, restrooms, camping, picnic area,

  On Oct 22, 1805 the expedition reached the falls, a long-time fishing area for many of the area tribes. At the arrival of Lewis and Clark, 17 lodges sat above the falls and 5 below. The corps camped two nights on the North bank below the falls. The falls are all but non-existent because of the dams. For further understanding of the loss of the falls to the tribes in the area, see this "storypath."

> Fishing
> At Celilo falls, native tribes regularly gathered to bring in huge quantities of fish with a complex structure used to catch the spawning fish. Once they were brought in, they were dried, pounded with stones into almost a powder, placed in salmon skin lined baskets that were then pressed in groups of twelve, weighted and preserved for several years into a kind of fish cake.

- **The Dalles Dam Visitor Center**, 3545 Bret Clodfelter Way, exit 87 from I84, 541-296-9778, call for tour and opening hours. Fish viewing, picnic areas, rose garden, scenic views.

- **Fort Dalles Museum**, 500 W 15th St, 541-296-4547, http://fortdallesmuseum.org/, 10-5. Local history in what was once a historic fort.

- **Rock Fort Campsite**, Bargeway Rd, Bridge and Garrison St. The campsite is along the rivertrail in Fort Dalles. Several interpretive panels describe the area, and as you read these you will be looking over the Columbia River and Oregon to the South. Climb up the rocks on the west side to view the actual campsite, which is in a basin you will see below. Wild flowers are often blooming in spring but be careful of snakes.

Clark stated, *"After a much needed respite from the arduous passage through Celilo Falls and the Long and Short Narrows of The Dalles, the expedition pushed off from Rock Fort on the morning of October 28, 1805, and began their entrance into the Columbia River Gorge. [October 28, 1805:] we proceeded on river inclosed on each Side in high Clifts of about 90 feet of loose dark coloured rocks."*

On Oct 25th 1805, the Corps made camp near this fort like outcropping staying for two days and three nights while they made celestial observations and fixed their battered canoes that had just survived the rapids of the Columbia River. The Chinookan tribes sent chiefs to visit the Corps while they were camped here. They also stopped here on their way home in April, 1806. The rocks are the familiar CRBG, and Clark noted the dramatic topographical changes notable as they passed through The Dalles area, *"we proceeded on, the mountains are high on each Side, containing Scattering pine white oake & under groth, hill Sides Steep and rockey"*

⌂ **Columbia Gorge Discovery Center**, 5000 Discovery Dr, 541-296-8600, https://www.gorgediscovery.org/, 9-5pm, closed major holidays, $9 adult, $4 youth, restrooms, café, nature trail, raptors, movie, geology exhibit.

This is a nice place to visit to learn about the Gorge. Limited Lewis and Clark exhibits but one hallway is devoted to the medical expertise of the expedition including descriptions of processes like bloodletting. For a general overview of the gorge history, culture and geology, this is an excellent choice. Extensive gift shop.

⌂ **Doug's Beach**, MP 79 Hwy. 14, Dallesport, 509-767-1159, 6:30-dusk, discover pass, one of the best windsurfing beaches around.

On Oct 29, 1805, Lewis and Clark stopped for supplies at an Indian Village of seven houses near the beach. They were fed and in return gave the Native women some ribbon. On the return trip, they attempted to trade for horses but were unsuccessful.

Hood River

I84 runs along the N side of this vibrant town. OR 35 comes in from the S on the W side of the town and US 30 runs right through town.

Take a break in Hood River. This is one of my favorite places to stay for a few days. The weather is temperate, the town has everything you need and it's centrally located. Several hotel chains, but the real winners here are the bed and breakfasts. **Seven Oaks** (1373 Barker Rd, https://www.sevenoaksbb.com/) or **Sakura Ridge** (5601 York Hill Dr, 541-386-2636, http://www.sakuraridge.com/) are good choices. Seven Oaks is off the beaten path, in a more peaceful area, in a handsome historical home. Sakura Ridge overlooks Mt Hood and orchards and herb gardens. **Hood River Bed and Breakfast** (918 Oak St, 541-387-2997. https://www.hoodriverbnb.com/) is just off downtown, has a deck with river views, and is great for walkability.

Lots of food choices. Walk downtown and check out the menus. **Solstice Wood Fire Pizza** (501 Portway Ave, 541-436-0800, http://solsticewoodfirecafe.com/) is a good, casual choice. **Celilo Restaurant** (16 Oak St, 541-386-5710, https://www.celilorestaurant.com/) offers upscale Pacific Northwestern, a mix of the best that Oregon and Washington have to offer from fish to wine. Looking for food to feed the road trip? Try out **Boda's Kitchen** (404 Oak St, 541-386-9876, https://www.bodaskitchen.com/) which is a kind of deli/gourmet grocery with sandwiches like banh mi and chicken curry potpies.

Bike Map to the Pacific

+ **Hood River County History Museum**, 300 E Port Marina Dr, 541-386-6772, https://www.hoodriverhistorymuseum.org/, 11-4 Mon-Sat, $5.

   Changing exhibits present contemporary and local history. Walking tours are also available. An outdoor paddle wheel is from a 1901 Steamer.

⌂ **Memaloose State Park**, I84 exit says Memaloose Rest Area and the park itself is only accessible going Westbound, 541-478-3008, camping, restrooms

   On Oct 29, 1805, Lewis and Clark called it "the Sepulchar Island". Chinook Indians used the island to burn their dead. Lower Memloose trailhead is on the S side of I84, accessible from the east bound Memloose Rest Area. Both traffic and train noise.

✦ **Columbia River Gorge National Scenic Area Office**, 902 Wasco Ave, Suite 200, 541-308-1700, map of area,

The Columbia River Gorge National Scenic Area protects the Columbia River for 80 miles along both the Washington and Oregon side. The fires in 2017 closed some of the falls and parking areas along the route. Call ahead before visiting this area.

🏛 **Tom McCall Preserve/Rowena Plateau**, Old Columbia River Scenic Hwy US 30, 11m E of Hood River, trails

Where the foothills of the Cascades meet with the drylands of the Columbia Plateau, this park has a one-mile trail through prairie, oak groves and ponds to a view of the Klickitat River. A longer trail is also accessible. Wildflowers in the spring are incredible. Lewis and Clark probably hiked in this very same area.

Stevenson

A rustic small town with a park along the river on WA 14. Stevenson feels kind of like Alaska with forests and water everywhere. Full services. The Corps set up camp in Oct 1805 near Stevenson.

Forest Service Information Center at Skamania Lodge, 131 SW Skamania Lodge Way, 509-427-2528, www.skamania.com

In the lobby of this resort, is a forest service information center with maps, books and guidance.

🏛 **Columbia Gorge Interpretive Center**, 900 SW Rock Creek Dr, 509-427-8211, http://www.columbiagorge.org/, 9-5pm, closed Major Holidays, $10 adult, $6 children, multi-media presentation

Center overlooks the river and includes some Lewis and Clark exhibits. One exhibit, "Clahclehlah and the Corridor of Commerce", focuses on how Lewis and Clark are viewed according to Native American oral history. Natural history and human history. Large fish wheel is the main exhibit. But the museum also has the largest collection of rosaries. The fish wheel was created by Tiffany studios in NY. Walkable from downtown.

Take a break at the **Skamania Lodge** (1131 SW Skamania Lodge Way, 844-432-4748, https://www.destinationhotels.com/skamania/resort) a gorgeous full-service resort set above the town with expansive gardens and lovely "tree houses" in the forest. Views over the gorge. One of the nicest hotels in the area. For a local meal with river views, head to **Clark & Lewies** (130 SW Cascade Ave, 509-219-0097, http://www.clarkandlewies.com/) a fun, lively place for lunch or dinner. Food is interesting and goes a step beyond the usual. Order Beer Cheese soup served with popcorn, the buffalo burger or fresh cod fish and chips.

Cascade Locks and Bradford Island

Bradford Island is accessible from WA on WA14, W of Hood River and accessible from OR on I84.

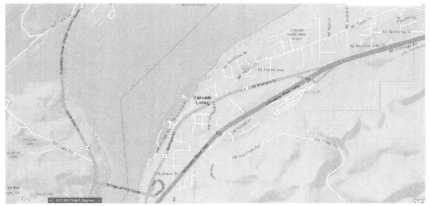

The portage for the corps here on April 11, 1806 was over a slippery, narrow trail, and they had to do it in the rain. Clark managed to bring up four of the canoes. Meanwhile, the Indians were stealing from them and Shields had to pull a knife to keep them from stealing a dog. They did manage to steal Seaman, but Lewis sent his crew after them with orders to get the dog even if it required killing Indians. The corps was clearly fed up at this point in the trip between the weather, the terrain and the pesky Indians.

Make a Day of It, Start in Stevenson at the Columbia Gorge Interpretive Center. Head across the Bridge of the Gods being sure to take time to stop underneath and check out the murals. Then head N on Wa Na Pa St and turn into the Marine Park. Enjoy lunch at Thunder Island Brewing Co. Visit the Cascade Locks Museum and then walk N in the park to stop at Sacagawea Circle to see the statue. Finish your visit with a tour of the Columbia Gorge Sternwheeler.

🏛 **Bradford Island Visitor Center at Bonneville Dam**, Star Route, Cascade Locks, 541-374-8820, http://www.nwp.usace.army.mil/bonneville/, trails, two visitor centers, one in Washington (see below) and Bradford Island in Oregon, 9-5pm, exhibits. The Dam was completed in 1938 and inundated the Great Rapids around which Lewis and Clark portaged. Interpretive signs on Lewis and Clark's visit on April 9, 1806. History and wildlife exhibits.

Washington Shore Visitor Complex, WA 14 to MP 38.5, turn S onto the Dam Access Rd following the signs to the visitor complex. Tours of the powerhouse, exhibits on electricity and hydroelectric dams.

The Corps stopped here on April 9, 1806 and camped on the island.

Fort Cascades Loop, just west of the dam, 1.5m, self-guided hike includes a fish wheel, views of the dam and of the Columbia river.

Ordway wrote on April 9, 1806, " *a number of these natives are moveing up to the Big Shoote (Cascades of the Columbia River) to fish... we halted at a village at the foot of the 1st rapid,... we purchased 2 fat dogs and crossed over to the South Shore and Camped*"

🏛 **Cascade Locks Marine Park**, 355 Wa Na Pa St, 541-374-8619, playground, picnic tables, restrooms, camping, interpretive signs, trail, Sacagawea statues, museum, mural on The Bridge of the Gods.

The Sacagawea statues were created by artist Heather Soderberg and dedicated in 2011. Both feature Sacagawea and Seaman. As you drive across the Cascade Locks bridge, it's hard to imagine the falls that were here when Lewis and Clark portaged around the area.

> Take a break on the **Columbia Gorge Sternwheeler** (299 NW Portage Rd, 503-224-3900, http://www.portlandspirit.com/) for a fun dining excursion on a boat. This is more about the experience than the food. Reserve online for a combination gorge cruise and brunch or dinner.

🏕 **Beacon Rock State Park**, 34841 WA 14, 509-427-8265, 8am-dusk, camping, restrooms, picnic tables, interpretive panels, fishing, 13m of bike and horse trails, trails can be closed due to Peregrine falcon nesting. Discover pass. Map.

1.7m switchback Hiking trail 848ft to rock provides great views of gorge, most of the trail is paved and includes interpretive panels on history and geology. The River to Rock trail also provides a one mile accessible trail at Doestch Day use area (WA 14 to Doetsch Ranch Rd) to Beacon Rock.

On Oct 31, 1805, Clark noted this geological formation as he was scouting a portage route around the Cascades. He wrote, "a remarkable high detached rock Stands in a bottom on the Stard Side . . . about 800 feet high and 400 paces around, we call the Beaten rock". On the return journey on April 6, 1806, they changed the name to "Beacon" Rock. This is also where Clark noted the tide was affecting the water levels making the corps believe they were actually a bit closer to the ocean than they were.

Beacon rock is gray basaltic andesite, a lighter basalt from typical CRBG basalts, and is quite young, comparatively, only 57,000 years old. The Missoula floods carved the formation by stripping away less-resistant volcanic ejecta. The rock stands today as one of the most noticeable landmarks the corps encountered. It's visible from both the surrounding cliffs and the river.

Corbett, OR

S of US30 on Corbett Hill Rd.

+ **Vista House at Crown Point State Park**, 40700 Historic Columbia River Hwy, Corbett, 503-695-2240 or 503-344-1368, http://www.vistahouse.com/, 9am-6pm, gift and coffee shop

    Great views of the Columbia River and of Rooster Rock.

⚑ **Rooster Rock State Park**, exit 25 I84, N, 800-551-6949, 503-695-2261, 6am-10pm, day use fee, picnic tables, restrooms, swimming (separate, clothing optional beach), trails, interpretive signs, Columbia Gorge Express,

    The corps camped nearby on Nov 2, 1805. This basalt rock formation is a landslide from the Crown Point rock formation.

⚑ **Blue Lake Regional Park**, 21224 NE Blue Lake Rd, 503-665-6918, 8am-sunset, $5 parking fee, picnic tables, restrooms, boat rental, fishing, playground, discovery garden, disc golf, 2-mile loop trail, wetland, sculptures at the west end of the lake. Field guide and map.

    The remains of a Chinook Village on-site on the Western end of the lake includes an interpretive plaque that explains how the Nichawqwli assisted Lewis and Clark in April, 1806. The Nichawqwli provided help in drawing a map and guided Clark to the Willamette River. Clark's party explored the Willamette on April 3, 1806. Clark used his "magic" in an Indian Village when they refused to trade with the corps. He used a magnet to move the needle of his compass and burned a match. The Indians were either impressed or frightened, and gave them all the food they wanted.

Cottonwood Beach, Washougal WA

Just S of WA 14 along the Columbia River.

Lewis and Clark passed today's Washougal on Nov 3, 1805. In 1806, the corps stayed for 6 nights at Cottonwood Beach for 6 nights.

⚑ **Captain William Clark Park/Cottonwood Beach**, S Index St at S 32nd St, 360-397-2285, 7am-dusk, restrooms, picnic tables, interpretive panels, trail, Map,

    The Corps camped for six days on March 31, 1806 and traded with local Indians at Cottonwood Beach. The Corps stayed as long as it took them to gather a store of meat. They also traveled down the Columbia to locate the Willamette River.

- ⌂ **Two Rivers Heritage Museum**, 1 Durgan St, 360-835-8742, http://www.2rhm.com/uncategorized/lewis-and-clark/, 11-3 Thurs-Sat.

  See a replica canoe that the corps used and watch a movie on the expedition. Other exhibits include a one-room schoolhouse and a hand-tool exhibit.

- ⚑ **Columbia River Dike Trail**, E of Washougal starting at Steamboat Landing Park (S 15th St, restrooms) and going through Cottonwood Beach to the Steigerwald Lake National Wildlife Refuge (WA 14 just after MM 18, Gate 6), trail follows the Columbia for 3.5m for a total of 6.4m

> Take a break in nearby Camas at the **Camas Hotel** (405 NE 4th Ave, 360-209-7522, http://www.camashotel.com/) an 107 year old inn with understated Victorian décor and wide variety of room styles and amenities. **Hidden River Roasters** (536 NE 5th Ave, 888-661-6612) has great coffee and pastries.

- ⚑ **Washougal River Greenway Trail**, starts at Baz Riverfront Park (NE 3rd loop) and ends at Yale St and NE 2nd Ave. trailhead. 2.2m crosses the Washougal River. Map.

- ⚑ **Steigerwald Lake National Wildlife Refuge**, WA 14 E mm 18, 5:30am-9pm, free, restrooms, interpretive panels, Map.

  Gibbons Creek Wildlife Art Trail, open May 1-Sept 30, 2.75m trail, this is a really cool trail that even kids will like. Interesting art work is installed throughout the trail.

Troutdale

US30 runs right through town.

- ⌂ **Multnomah Falls Visitor Center**, 53000 E Historic Columbia River Hwy, Bridal Veil, 15m E of Troutdale off I84, 503-695-2372, www.multnomahfallslodge.com, 9-5, trails, restrooms, snack bar, restaurant. Map. A shuttle provides transport between other parking areas and Multnomah falls. See www.ColumbiaGorgeExpress.com.

  On our recent visit, the visitor center was more packed than usual. Fires in 2017 closed parts of the Gorge Scenic road and several of the waterfalls, resulting in Multnomah being visited more than usual. Be prepared for crowds. In a regular year, this visitor center gets over 2 million visitors (the most of any natural recreation site in the Pacific Northwest). The falls result from underground springs from Larch Mountain.

Lewis and Clark noted the falls in their notebooks. On October 30, 1805, Lewis wrote,

"passed Several places where the rocks projected into the river & have the appearance of having separated from the mountains and fallen into the river, small niches are formed in the banks below those projecting rocks which is common in this part of the river, Saw 4 Cascades caused by Small Streams falling from the mountains on the Lard. October 30, 1805". *Journals of the Lewis and Clark Expedition*. University of Nebraska–Lincoln. Retrieved December 23, 2017."

⛫ **Lewis and Clark State Recreation Site/ Sandy River Delta**, 1 Jordan Rd, Troutdale, 800-551-6949, 6am-10pm, picnic tables, swimming, interpretive panels, botanical trail, bird blind overlooks the delta

The corps called this area "the quicksand" when they camped and explored here in Nov, 1805. The name quickly morphed into "The Sandy", and is now the name of the town "Sandy". The Bird Blind is part of the Confluence Project, by Maya Lin and it commemorates the bird species of the Lewis and Clark expedition. Each slats of black locust wood has the name of one of the bird species Lewis and Clark recorded.

⛫ **Dabney State Park**, 30436 Historic Columbia River Hwy, E of Troutdale, 800-551-6949, 6am-10pm, picnic tables, swimming, fishing,

Sergeant Pryor and two men ascended the Quicksand River (now The Sandy), interpretive sign.

Take a break at **Tad's Chicken 'n Dumplins** (1325 E Historic Columbia River Hwy., 503-666-5337, http://tadschicdump.com/) which comes highly recommended from the locals. It opened as a roadhouse in the 1920's and still holds the wood-paneled charm of that era. Views over the Troutdale Bridge. And, stay the night at **McMenamins Edgefield** (2126 SW Halsey St, 503-669-8610, https://www.mcmenamins.com/edgefield), once the local poor farm and now a venue for life music and attractive gardens.

Portland/Vancouver Area

⌂ **Oregon Historical Society and History Center**, 1200 SW Park Ave, Portland, 503-222-1741, website, 10-5pm

Expedition artifacts and library with significant books on the expedition. 8-story trompe l'oeil murals depict the expedition members. New exhibit to open in Feb 2019 that will include an overview of the state's history.

⌂ **Lewis and Clark College, Aubrey Watzek Library**, 615 SW Palatine Hill Rd,   503-768-7270, http://digitalcollections.lclark.edu/exhibits/show/lewis---clark-expedition-colle/about-the-collections, holds the largest collection of books and ephemera relating to the expedition. Statue of York.

⌂ **Government Island State Recreation Area**, 7005 NE Marine Dr, 503-281-0944, accessible only by boat, hiking, fishing, camping. Lewis and Clark camped on the north side of the island Nov 3, 1805. Clark called it "Dimond" island.

✦ **Fort Vancouver National Historic Site**, 1501 E Evergreen Blvd, Vancouver, 360-816-6230, https://www.nps.gov/fova/index.htm, visitor center, interpretive panels

Focus of the fort is on the fur trade and Buffalo Soldiers. Fort overlooks the area where the corps traveled.

✦ **Clark County Historical Museum**, 1511 Main St, Vancouver, 360-993-5679, http://www.cchmuseum.org/, 11-4, closed Sun-Mon, $5 adults, $4 students, walking tours

Local and Native American history.

✿ **Cathedral Park**, 6905 N. Philadelphia Ave, interpretive signs.

Clark camped nearby with eight men on April 2, 1806. It had long been a main fishing area for the Native Americans. Park is underneath St Johns Bridge where commuters zoom along above.

✦ **Kelley Point Park**, 8484 N Kelley Point Park Rd, 503-823-2223, 6am-9pm, city park once obscured the entrance to the Willamette River, picnic areas, hiking, biking, swimming, canoeing, interpretive signs

The confluence of the Willamette and the Columbia. It's the westernmost tip of Portland.

♀ **Sauvie Island**, Hwy 30 Sauvie Island Bridge 10m N of Portland, parking permit $7, porta-potties, hiking, biking, swimming, bird-watching, interpretive sign. Map.

Multnomah, flathead Indians, inhabited the island when Lewis and Clark visited in 1805 and 1806. They named it "Wappatoe". They camped across the Columbia from the island.

Lewis wrote,

"Wappatoe Island is … high and extreemly fertile … with ponds which produce great quantities of the … bulb of which the natives call wappatoe … we passed several fishing camps on Wappetoe island …"

✿ **Confluence Land Bridge**, Vancouver, 1109 E 5th St, access from Columbia Way Blvd at Old Apple Tree Park, or from the N side from I5 take the Mill Plain Blvd east exit and turn right at Fort Vancouver Way to East 5th st, 360-693-0123,

The bridge commemorates the history of the Vancouver area including the Lewis and Clark expedition. The bridge provides interpretive information about native plants many of which Lewis and Clark identified. The site marks a historically significant crossroads for all Americans.

Ridgefield, WA

N of Vancouver WA

✿ **Ridgefield National Wildlife Refuge**, 2 entrance stations (the Carty unit is where the plankhouse is located-see below), the River S Unit is accessed off 9th Av to S Hillhurst St., 5:30am-9pm, $3 passenger vehicle, restrooms, trails, auto tour. Map.

Preserves the Cathlapotle town site where the expedition visited Nov 5, 1805 and again on March 29, 1806. Clark noted that the birds flying in the area disturbed his sleep. They met with the Cathlapotle to trade. The area had long been occupied. Archaeological excavation indicates the area has hosted humans for at least 2300 years. The Cathlapotle build large cedar plank lodges, woven baskets and carved wooden objects. The corps camped at a riverbank site, Carty Lake. Auto tour on itunes, on website.

>**Cathlapotle Plankhouse/Carty Unit**, 28908 NW Main St, 360-887-4106, https://ridgefieldfriends.org/plankhouse/, weekends May 5-Oct 7, 12-4, restrooms, trails.

>The plankhouse, built following archaeological findings, is regularly used but is also open to visitors. Volunteers provide tours and answer questions. The corps camped here in Nov. 1805 and in March 1806.

Fairview, OR

I94 runs through Fairview which is on the Columbia River.

- **Blue Lake Regional Park**, 20500 NE Marine Dr, 503-797-1850, swimming, boating, picnicking, hiking, playground, $5 day use.

  >The Chinook tribe have been coming to this region for centuries. Clark met with the Nichaqwli here in April, 1806. The Indians gave Clark needed information about the Willamette river and about how smallpox had affected the local tribes.

- **Chinook Landing Marine Park**, 22300 NE Marine Dr., 503-665-4995, $5 day use fee, restrooms, picnic area, boating, archery, fishing

Rainier, OR

US 30 runs through town on the banks of the Columbia.
Lewis and Clark came through this area in November, 1805 and in March, 1806.

- **Prescott Beach County Park**, 73125 Prescott Beach, 5m S of Rainier OR, 503-566-2128, sunrise-sunset, fishing, windsurfing, picnic shelter, playground, interpretive signs.

  >Corps camped under a point of high ground which is probably at nearby Laurel Beach on Nov 5, 1805.

- **Deer Island**, Hwy 30, interpretive sign overlooks the private island where the corps visited twice in Nov 1805 and March 28th 1806 and killed several deer.

  >Clark wrote

"... This morning we Set out verry early and at 9 A. M. arived at an old Indian Village on the N E side of Deer island where we found our hunters had halted and left one man with the Canoes at their Camp, they arrived last evening at this place, and Six of them turned out very early to hunt ..."

Skamokawa, WA

WA 4 on the Columbia River.

Chief Skamokawa, of the Wahkiakum tribe, met with Lewis and Clark while they were wintering in nearby Fort Clatsop on Dec. 29, 1805.

- **Vista Park**, 13 Vista Park Rd, 360-795-8605, 7am-dusk, restrooms, camping, Yurts, swimming, interpretive signs on Lewis and Clark

  Wahkiakum Indian village occupied an area near the park when Lewis and Clark visited on Nov 7, 1805. The area had been inhabited as long as 2300 years ago.

- **Redman Hall River Life Interpretive Center**, 1394 W State Rt 4, 360-795-3007, https://www.friendsofskamokawa.org/, Thurs-Sun 12-4.

  Historical and cultural displays, and great views of the Columbia River from the third floor bell tower.

Take a break at the **Duck Inn** (1377 W WA 4, 360-795-6055) for a tasty lunch or breakfast with a club sandwich, coleslaw and fries. Take a seat on the deck and enjoy the view. Stay the night across the street at the **Skamokawa Resort** (1391 W WA 4, 360-795-0726, https://www.skamokawaresort.com/home-1.html) which offers 8 hotel rooms and several cabins. Rooms are simple but offer good views and a simple, peaceful setting. **Twin Gables** (1416 WA 4, 360-795-3942, https://twingables.net/) is another good lodging choice with New England Charm. There are only two rooms in the inn but it's a full service property and makes for a good base for exploration.

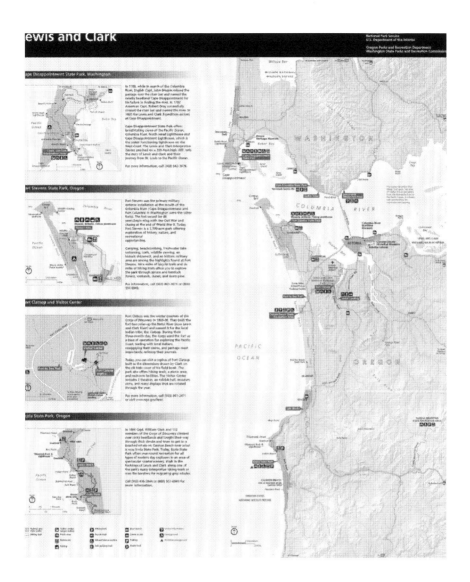

Cathlamet, WA

WA 4 runs on the E side of the city which sits on the Columbia River.

When Lewis and Clark traveled in this area in Nov 1805, they noted many abandoned Chinook villages, most likely the victims of smallpox introduced by earlier fur traders and visitors. Lewis and Clark located the Wahkiakums and traded with them. The Kathlamet Indians, a Chinnok tribe, also lived here.

- **Julia Butler Hansen Wildlife Refuge**, from I5 take the Longview exit to Cathlamet and contine 1m to Steamboat Slough Rd, turn left, 360-765-

3915, sunrise-sunset, office is open 7:30-4 Mon-Fri., boating, fishing, hunting, trails. Brochure. Call about access, floods can shut down the entrance road to cars though pedestrians and bikers can still enter.

Lewis and Clark traveled through the refuge in Nov. 1805. They were the first white men to note the abundant Columbian White Tailed deer. On their return trip, they hunted on Deer Island in March 1806.

Clark wrote,

"....two Canos of Indians met and returned with us to their village which is Situated... behind a cluster of Marshey Islands, on a narrow chanl of the river through which we passed to village of 4 Houses...." Today those marshy islands are known as the Hunting Islands.

Lewis and Clark National Wildlife Refuge, 46 Steamboat Slough Rd, 360-795-3915, headquarters 7:30-4 Mon-Fri, access only by boat from Skamokawa Vista Park by Hwy 4 (In Oregon from John Day County Park or Aldrich Point), brochure

35,000 acres of mudflats, tidal marshes and islands that have changed very little since Lewis and Clark visited the area.

Knappton, WA
US 101 over the Astoria Bridge and E on WA 401

Knappton Cove Heritage Center, 521 WA 402, 503-738-5206, http://www.knapptoncoveheritagecenter.org/,

Certain summer weekends enactors act out the Lewis & Clark expedition. See the website for dates.

Dismal Nitch, 230 WA 401, interpretive signs

Lewis and Clark had arrived almost to the end of the Columbia and were attempting to get around the point near Astoria. But the water was so rough, it was impossible. They camped on the moving logs as they attempted to round the point over the course of several days. Around the 4th day, they were finally able to accomplish the feat when the water calmed briefly. They called this area, "dismal nitch". The nitches referred to the series of coves in the area.

Great views of the Columbia River and the Astoria-Megler Bridge.

Clark wrote, *"As our situation became Seriously dangerous, we took the advantage of a low tide & moved our Camp around a point a Short distance to a Small wet bottom at the mouth of a Small Creek (Megler Creek), which we had observed when we first came to this cove..."*

❡ **Middle Village Station Camp**, 345 US 101, 503-861-4414

Lewis and Clark stayed here 10 days once they got away from Dismal Nitch from Nov 15-25, 1805. They used the area as a base to explore the surrounds. The Chinook lived her for centuries because the location provided food, game and shelter materials. The waterway here was highly traveled for trade.

On Nov. 18, Clark and some of the men hiked to Cape Disappointment, mapping and recording what they viewed including a California Condor.

Today, St Mary's Catholic church, built in 1904, is on site, some canoes and a nature viewing area. Washington State parks hoped to create a more extensive visitor experience. Archaeologists conducted a dig and found extensive evidence of early Chinook settlement but also native remains. The identification of the remains led to the decision to do only minimal development in this area.

❡ **Fort Columbia State Park and Chinook Point**, US 101, 360-777-8221, restroom, 5m of hiking trails, bird watching, picnic tables, interpretive center (July 1- Sept 5 11-4).

The Corps had their first glimpse of the Pacific Ocean near Chinook Point on Nov. 15, 1805. They build temporary shelters here with boards from an apparently deserted Chinook village and settled in for ten days as they explored the surrounding area. The group voted on where to camp because the current site did not have enough game and decided to move S to Fort Clatsop where they believed the game would be more plentiful.

Today, this is one of the best preserved Forts in the western US with 12 intact historical fort buildings.

❡ **Fort Clatsop/Lewis and Clark National Historical Park**, 92343 Fort Clatsop Rd, 4.5m SW of Astoria, 503-861-2471, https://www.nps.gov/lewi/planyourvisit/fortclatsop.htm, park is open every day. Events are offered throughout the year. Visitor center, restrooms, paddle tours (register here), nature trail with interpretive panels of the plants seen by Lewis and Clark, 6-mile fort to sea trail. Excellent bookstore, probably the best for Lewis and Clark books. Selection of jewelry, posters and post cards as well. Map.

Exhibits focus on the different tasks of the exhibition. They also include a list of all the exhibition participants, their jobs and what happened to them when they left. If you are only going to get to one

Lewis and Clark site in Oregon, I highly recommend this one for it interpretive exhibits, outdoor replica fort and the bookstore.

The Corps built Fort Clatsop starting in Dec. 1805 with two rows of huts separated by a parade ground to winter in. They left the area on March 23, 1806. The current fort is a replica. Lewis and Clark started out on the North side of the Columbia but after asking the corps what they thought, the group decided to winter on the south side because they believed if would have better access to meat. They endured almost three months straight of dismal, rainy weather. The meat they killed spoiled quickly.

When they departed from the fort, the group made a significant change: Lewis and Clark decided to break up the group so they could investigate further afield. Lewis would head east to Great Falls and explore the Marias River to find its northern reaches. In the Louisiana purchase, the US was given all the land that the Missouri and its tributaries feed. The Marias, as one of the tributaries, might provide additional land for the US.

Clark would head SE to Camp Fortunate and then down the Beaverhead and Jefferson to the three forks of the Missouri. Part of his party would continue on to meet Lewis at the Great Falls while Clark continued on the Yellowstone and make contact with additional Indian tribes.

In their first winter, the corps made easy friends of the Mandan Indians. But this was not the case at Fort Clatsop. The Clatsop and Chinook Indians regularly interacted with the corps through trading and sharing food, but the corps did not welcome them into the fort. And, the journals suggest a general level of distrust. The coastal Indians were wily traders and not easily impressed into parting with their goods without a good return. And, the rule at the fort was that all natives must be outside the palisades by nightfall. It was a long, hard, wet and largely unfriendly winter. The corps couldn't wait for it to end.

⌂ **Sunset Beach State Recreation Area,** US 101 MP 13 to Sunset Beach Rd, 503-861-3170, restrooms, hiking

This park marks the west trailhead of the Fort to sea trail from Fort Clatsop. This is a rare opportunity to walk in Lewis and Clark's footsteps.

⌂ **The Lewis and Clark Trail – Travois Rd**, crosses Hwy. 12 at Pataha Creek, 5m E of Pomeroy. This quarter mile is the last part of the once much longer Indian trail.

The road was used frequently by the Nez Perce, Walla Walla and Cayuse people as a transit between the Walla Walla River and the confluence of the Snake and Clearwater Rivers. A travois was often used along the trail and the poles dragged over the trail left persistent markings.

Ilwaco

Following US 101 almost to the Pacific, Ilwaco is right before Cape Disappointment at the end of the peninsula (see Columbia Gorge map above).

♀ **Cape Disappointment State Park**, 244 Robert Gray Dr, located where the Columbia River meets the Pacific, 360-642-3078, https://parks.state.wa.us/486/Cape-Disappointment, 6:30am-dusk, discovery pass, camping, restrooms, café at the entrance, discovery trail, walking trails through forests and along the coast, lighthouse, Maya Lin confluence project, summer concert series (see website for dates).

Large state park of almost 2000 acres on the Pacific offers 27miles of beach and two lighthouses in addition to the interpretive center (see below). Lewis and Clark came through this area.

Lewis and Clark Interpretive Center at Cape Disappointment Long Beach, 244 Robert Gray Dr. SW, perched on the cliff at the end of the cape, 360-642-3029, 10-5 Apr-Sept, Wed–Sun rest of the year, $5 adult, $2.50 children.

Exhibits offer an overview of the Corps' journey with a focus on the discoveries along the Columbia River including clothing, equipment and what they discovered. Murals depict the corps timeline. Patrick Glass' published journal is on view. Movie on Lewis and Clark, exhibits on Jefferson's influence. 2nd floor includes historic exhibits after the expedition. Recommended.

> **Lewis and Clark Discovery Trail**, Beard's Hollow parking area, 8m one way paved, goes between Long Beach and Ilwaco, bikes, walking. Trail passes a gray whale skeleton and sculpture and sculptures of William Clark including one with a sturgeon.

✦ **Columbia Pacific Heritage Museum**, near Clark's trail, 115 SE Lake St, 360-642-3446, http://columbiapacificheritagemuseum.org/, 10-4pm Tues-Sat, $5 adult, $4

Native American, Pioneer and European Exploration exhibits.

Astoria, OR

US 30 and 101 come together in Astoria located at a peninsula on the Columbia River. The Astoria Megler Bridge takes you N into Washington.

✦ **Columbia River Maritime Museum**, 1792 Marine Dr, 503-325-2323, http://www.crmm.org/, 9:30-5, $14 adult, $5 children.

Large museum with a variety of exhibits on the Maritime History of the area from Native American uses to the Coast Guard to the more than 200 ship wrecks. Visitors can also tour a US Navy Destroyer. If you have an interest in Maritime history, this is an excellent museum.

⌂ **Astoria Column**, 1 Coxcomb Dr, 503-325-2963, https://astoriacolumn.org/, panoramic viewpoint. Go to the gift shop and purchase a biplane and then climb the tower and toss the plane out.

The winds up here tend to take the biodegradable planes for a long ride. Check out the interpretive panels that highlight different Lewis and Clark sites viewable from this highpoint above Astoria. Adventurous walkers can walk up to the column from Astoria and then climb the tower steps for a strenuous workout.

Take a break at **Salt Pub and Hotel** (147 Howerton Ave, 360-642-7258, https://salt-hotel.com/), a good place for food and lodging. Attractive, simple, modern rooms overlook the harbor, and meals feature local and seasonal food.

Youngs River Falls Park, 88450 Youngs River Rd, Youngs river loop off Hwy. 202, 8m S of Astoria, trail, picnic area

In March 1806 the Corps discovered these 50ft falls while Patrick Gass and a hunting party were seeking game. Pretty undeveloped so you can almost feel what it must have been like for Gass and his crew to come across this fall. If you visit in summer, expect swimming crowds.

⌂ **Twilight Creek Eagle Sanctuary**, E Columbia River Hwy, 2.5m E of Astoria, 503-325-9306, trails, interpretive signs.

Viewing platform for the Wildlife refuge. Lewis and Clark's campsite on Nov. 26, 1805 was a few miles downstream of the sanctuary.

Hammond, OR
US 101 to OR 104 N.

⌂ **Fort Stevens State Park and Museum**, 100 Peter Iredale Rd, US 101 N from Astoria to OR 104 N, 503-861-2471, camping, cabins, yurts, swimming, 9-miles of biking trails and 6-miles of hiking, fishing, canoeing, historic civil war earthworks and WWII gun batteries. Military museum, guided tours, interpretive displays

Clark notes that there was a Clatsop settlement here. Today, a replica of the settlement offers living history demonstrations.

⌂ **Bradley State Scenic Wayside**, 46975 US 30, 503-861-3170, restrooms, picnic areas

Great river views. This is where Lewis and Clark paddled in Nov, 1805, and you can too.

preservation and seasoning. Almost starving on the trip West, the corps knew they had to have preserved food to carry with them.

Cannon Beach, OR
US 101 runs along the E side of town, the Pacific on the W.
Cannon Beach Visitor Center, 2nd and Spruce, 10-5pm.

⌂ **Ecola Creek/Cannon Beach**, 5th St head N on Ecola Park Rd to the fee station, 503-436-2844, restrooms, camping, hiking, interpretive signs, 2.5m Clatsop loop trail, Map.

Just south of this site, the expedition came to see a beached whale on Jan 5, 1806. Clark bartered for 300 pounds of blubber. Follow the loop trail to step into Clark and Sacagawea's footsteps. The 2.5m Clatsop Loop trail follows part of the whale-finding route. Cliffside view points.

⌂ Cannon Beach History Center, 1387 Spruce St, 503-436-9301, https://cbhistory.org/, 11-5.

The history of Cannon Beach, Native American Coastal Indians, and an interpretive exhibit that includes Lewis and Clark's expedition.

Seaside, OR

US 101 N.

🏛 **Seaside Museum and Historical Center**, 570 Necanicum Dr, 503-738-7065, https://www.seasideoregonmuseum.com/, 10-3, closed Sun.

Native American exhibits including one that explores the Clatsop interaction with Lewis and Clark. Another exhibit shows how the expedition mined salt from the ocean. Many other historical exhibits.

⚲ **The Salt Works Historic Site**, US 101 and Ave G to Beach Drive W then left to Lewis and Clark way, foot of Broadway street, interpretive signs.

Reconstructed salt works oven replicates the one the Corps used to boil seawater for salt Jan-Feb 1806. The corps built a furnace to produce the salt which they used for food

Picture and Map Credits

All maps of the Lewis and Clark Trail come from the National Park Service.

All other maps, unless otherwise noted, are from the USGS, https://viewer.nationalmap.gov/advanced-viewer/.

All pictures are the property of the author unless otherwise noted and cannot be used without permission.

Quoted Material

Quotes throughout the text come from the Journals of the Lewis and Clark Expedition, the University of Nebraska, https://lewisandclarkjournals.unl.edu/.

Appendix 1 Scavenger Hunt

Use this list for a scavenger hunt. I've left extra spaces to add your own items as well.

Items	Where located	Use for what?
Transportation		
keelboat		
dugout canoe		
bullboat		
Pirogue		
Native American		
native american earth lodge		
native american tipi		
Places		
columbia river		
marias river		
continental divide		
yellowstone river		
Animals		
otter		
muskrat		
bison		
People		
statue of Lewis		
statue of clark		
statue of Sacagawea		
States of sacagawea with pomp		
statue of three or more members of the group		
Seaman		
Tools		
Air gun		
Battle axe		
Capote		
quadrant		
compass		

Flora/Plants		
Camas		
Prickly Pear		
Wappato		

Printed in Great Britain
by Amazon

34822389R00087